GOSPEL HOPE

in Pregnancy and Infant Loss

KRISTYN PEREZ

Gospel Hope in Pregnancy and Infant Loss
Copyright © 2022 by The Daily Grace Co.
Hanover, Maryland. All rights reserved.

Quotes by David Powlison taken from *God's Grace in Your Suffering* by David Powlison, Copyright © 2018, pp. 16. Used by permission of Crossway, a publishing ministry of Good News Publishers, Wheaton, IL 60187, www.crossway.org.

Quotes by Elisabeth Elliot taken from *Keep a Quiet Heart* by Elisabeth Elliot, Copyright 2012. Revell, imprint of Baker Publishing Group, http://bakerpublishinggroup.com.

Unless otherwise noted, all Scripture quotations are taken from the Christian Standard Bible®, Copyright © 2020 by Holman Bible Publishers. Used by permission. Christian Standard Bible® and CSB® are federally registered trademarks of Holman Bible Publishers.

The Daily Grace Co. exists to equip disciples to know and love God and His Word by creating beautiful, theologically rich, and accessible resources so that God may be glorified and the gospel made known.

Designed in the United States of America and printed in China.

*God longs to comfort
you, heal and help you.*

Table of Contents

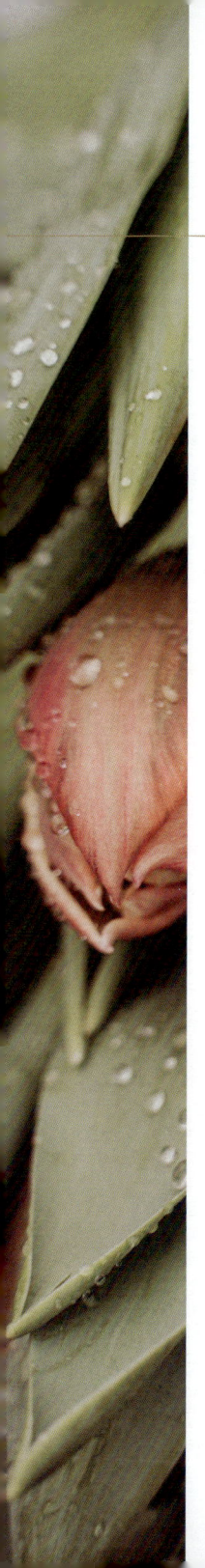

1. **WHAT IS MISCARRIAGE, STILLBIRTH, OR INFANT LOSS?** 6

   What is Miscarriage, Stillbirth, or Infant Loss? 8

   A Common Struggle: *Stats* 9

   A Common Struggle: *In the Bible* 15

   Common Responses 16

   A Note on Triggers 18

2. **HOPE FOR TODAY** 22

   God is With You 24

   God Will Help You 25

   God Will Make All Things Right 34

3. **MOURNING YOUR LOSS** 38

   Biblical Lament 40

   Be Honest With Your Emotions 44

   Honestly Evaluate Feelings of Guilt 47

   Understand Your Identity in Christ 50

   Biblical Community 54

   When God Says No: Trusting God in Suffering 58

   Find Hope in Scripture 60

   Planning a Ceremony to Grieve the Loss 63

   Have a Plan for Important Dates 68

4. **COMMON QUESTIONS** 72

   Where is God? 74

   Is God Punishing Me? 76

   Why Did God Allow This to Happen to Me? 80

Was My Unborn Baby a Real Person? 84

Where is the Baby Now? 86

Will This Happen Again? 90

Will the Pain Ever End? 94

5. FAMILY PLANNING AFTER PREGNANCY OR INFANT LOSS 100

Pregnancy After Miscarriage, Stillbirth, or Infant Loss 102

Adoption After Miscarriage, Stillbirth, or Infant Loss 106

Secondary Infertility 110

6. PROCESSING PREGNANCY OR INFANT LOSS WITH OTHERS 116

Show Grace 118

Guard Against Bitterness 122

Find Trusted Friends 126

Processing Pregnancy or Infant Loss With Your Children 130

Processing Pregnancy or Infant Loss With Your Spouse 137

7. HOW TO HELP THOSE WHO HAVE EXPERIENCED LOSS 142

Be a Friend 144

Pray 145

Offer Tangible Support 148

Mention the Baby's Name 150

What Not to Say 153

What to Say 156

8. HOPE FOR THE FUTURE 160

# 01.

What is Miscarriage, Stillbirth, or Infant Loss?

WHAT IS MISCARRIAGE,
STILLBIRTH, OR INFANT LOSS?

A COMMON STRUGGLE: *STATS*

A COMMON STRUGGLE:
IN THE BIBLE

COMMON RESPONSES

A NOTE ON TRIGGERS

WHAT IS MISCARRIAGE, STILLBIRTH, OR INFANT LOSS?

Joy. Exhilaration. Relief. Tears of happiness. Two pink lines across a tiny, white stick changed your world forever. You feel like you won the lottery. You'd never received such great news in your life, and you couldn't wait to share the news with family and friends. But weeks, or perhaps months later, the memory of this indescribable high was followed by a devastating low. Spotting. Cramps. Pain. They can't find a heartbeat. You lost the baby. The world blurs as you process the news of death dwelling inside your body.

To anyone picking up this booklet, either to process the loss of your own baby or to help someone who is grieving, a definition of pregnancy or infant loss may seem irritatingly obvious. You not only know what this kind of loss is, but you've felt its grief down to your bones. Yet sadly, in a culture that aims to blur the lines of when life begins, we must define terms. Medical doctors define a miscarriage as the loss of a pregnancy before twenty weeks. After twenty weeks, the loss of a pregnancy is called a stillbirth. When a baby passes away after being born, this is called an infant loss. Although there can be a myriad of causes and risk factors for pregnancy and infant loss—including age, drug use, sudden infant death syndrome (SIDS), and infections—many deaths don't come with an explanation. The loss of life, whatever its causes, can have devastating results.

Throughout this booklet, *we will point to a God who understands and draws near to us in our grief.*

He is the loving counselor, the compassionate friend, and the faithful Father. He does not rush you along in your pain but stays with you in it. At the same time, He is not content to leave you stuck in your brokenness and pain. Instead,

God longs to comfort you, heal you, and help you.

As we read the words of Scripture throughout this booklet, you can find comfort in the arms of a God who loves you, cares for you in your grief, and will provide every good thing you need.

A COMMON STRUGGLE: STATS

You look back and remember the waves of excitement or relief from a positive pregnancy test. Maybe you got pregnant easily. It was unexpectedly quick or maybe even a surprise. Or perhaps you've been on fertility medicine and seeking fertility treatments for years, and the positive pregnancy test was like cold, fresh water on your weary soul. But suddenly, the excitement ended. First, perhaps with apprehension: *Is this happening? Am I miscarrying?* And then with confirmation and shock: *How could this be happening?*

Or maybe, you had the joy of a beautiful delivery with your baby and were able to enjoy days or weeks or months with your child before she tragically passed. The pain of losing her feels as if a part of you has died. Your heart has been destroyed. All that remains is an empty crib, unworn onesies, and a pile of unused diapers.

Medical studies show that between ten and twenty percent of women who know that they are pregnant experience miscarriages. That means that the actual stats for miscarriage are likely much higher, as many women do not know that they're pregnant in the early weeks to report a miscarriage. Reports suggest that there are approximately twenty-three million miscarriages around the world each year, which translates into forty-four miscarriages a minute. Not only this, but about one in one hundred women experiences the loss of a baby after twenty weeks, which translates to roughly twenty-four thousand babies every year in the United States alone. Worldwide, the infant mortality rate varies greatly by country, ranging from 0.2–8.1 out of every one hundred children passing away before their first birthday. The numbers are staggering, heartbreaking, and mind-numbing.

But, while pregnancy and infant loss may be common, they are not commonplace. The enormity of these statistics does not lessen their painful blow when we lose a baby we love. Instead, let the vastness of these statistics be a reminder that you are not alone. Though this world is broken, there is a cloud of witnesses who have been through this painful road you now walk and who have found God to be faithful.

Thousands of women have found hope in a God who sustains, enters into their pain, and heals their wounds.

They have found comfort in the words of Scripture and hope in the arms of the Father. You are not alone in this struggle.

*Let the vastness
of these statistics
be a reminder that
you are not alone.*

Psalm 139

Lord, you have searched me and known me.
You know when I sit down and when I stand up;
you understand my thoughts from far away.
You observe my travels and my rest;
you are aware of all my ways.
Before a word is on my tongue,
you know all about it, Lord.
You have encircled me;
you have placed your hand on me.
This wondrous knowledge is beyond me.
It is lofty; I am unable to reach it.

Where can I go to escape your Spirit?
Where can I flee from your presence?
If I go up to heaven, you are there;
if I make my bed in Sheol, you are there.
If I fly on the wings of the dawn
and settle down on the western horizon,
even there your hand will lead me;
your right hand will hold on to me.
If I say, "Surely the darkness will hide me,
and the light around me will be night"—
even the darkness is not dark to you.
The night shines like the day;
darkness and light are alike to you.

For it was you who created my inward parts;
you knit me together in my mother's womb.

*I will praise you
because I have been remarkably and wondrously made.
Your works are wondrous,
and I know this very well.
My bones were not hidden from you
when I was made in secret,
when I was formed in the depths of the earth.
Your eyes saw me when I was formless;
all my days were written in your book and planned
before a single one of them began.*

*God, how precious your thoughts are to me;
how vast their sum is!
If I counted them,
they would outnumber the grains of sand;
when I wake up, I am still with you.*

*God, if only you would kill the wicked—
you bloodthirsty men, stay away from me—
who invoke you deceitfully.
Your enemies swear by you falsely.
Lord, don't I hate those who hate you,
and detest those who rebel against you?
I hate them with extreme hatred;
I consider them my enemies.*

*Search me, God, and know my heart;
test me and know my concerns.
See if there is any offensive way in me;
lead me in the everlasting way.*

Even through their sorrow, these saints in Scripture found comfort in God, who is merciful.

A COMMON STRUGGLE: *IN THE BIBLE*

Did you know that infertility, pregnancy and infant loss, and grief are all in the Bible? Because of the fall, women for centuries have walked the painful path of miscarriage and grieved the loss of their children. Some women in Scripture endured years of infertility, while others experienced the grief of losing their babies.

Consider Abraham and Sarah, who were almost one hundred years old before they had their first son, Isaac. Although God promised that their descendants would be as many as the stars in the sky, they remained month after month without any signs of pregnancy. We can only imagine the shame, disappointment, and bitterness Sarah experienced year after year as she lived in a culture that highly prized motherhood. Sarah's daughter-in-law, Rebekah, also identified with Sarah's struggles, as she endured barrenness for many years.

Sadly, the longings of Rebekah are not unique in Scripture. They are joined in the pages of the Bible with the cries of Rachel, Hannah, and Elizabeth—women who longed for children and cried out to the Lord throughout many years of disappointment. Not only did women experience infertility in the Bible, but some men and women also grieved the loss of their babies. After pleading to the Lord to save his child, King David grieved the loss of his baby in 2 Samuel 12. Miscarriages were also common throughout Israelite times as they were referenced in Exodus 21:22–23.

God did not choose to white out the pain of His people in the words of Scripture but included their names and stories in His Word. He counted their tears and comforted their grieving hearts. He recorded their stories and their sorrows, in part to help us find comfort today. Even through their sorrow, these saints in Scripture found comfort in God, who is merciful. Through lifted hands and tear-stained faces, they found that God was not oblivious or withdrawn in their pain; He was near. For centuries, God has sustained the faith of His people, even through the painful roads of pregnancy or infant loss. He has never abandoned His children, and He will not leave you now.

COMMON RESPONSES

Emptiness. Sadness. Despair. Anger. Denial. If you've experienced the loss of a child, you've likely experienced the gamut of emotions. Some days, you don't want to get out of bed. Other days, you want to get dressed up and pretend like nothing ever happened. Some days you're hopeful. Other days you're depressed or angry at God. These are all common emotional responses to grief.

Each person responds to the loss of their baby differently, even spiritually. While some Christians use their grief to press into their faith and cling to God for help, others question everything. Although the roller coaster of emotions after a pregnancy or infant loss can be overwhelming, you can rest in this:

through every emotion, thought, concern, and fear, you are not alone.

God, who sees our every thought, knows what you're feeling, and He longs to comfort you.

God is our help and mercy in our time of need.

You can talk to Him about every doubt and every emotion because He is compassionate and because He heals our wounds.

To be clear, not all pregnancies are planned. While every life is a gift, sometimes we weren't planning to add a new baby to our family. Perhaps the baby was conceived outside of marriage and felt like an act of judgment to you. Or perhaps life was already overwhelmingly busy as you juggled a full-time job, an absent spouse, and several young children. You couldn't imagine adding another baby to the mix, and then you lost the baby. You feel relieved. While this booklet will predominantly function within the framework of grieving mothers facing pregnancy or infant loss, we must acknowledge another truth: at times, the loss of a baby can bring with it varying emotions, such as relief. This does not necessarily mean that you didn't value the baby's life. Sometimes the timing of an unplanned pregnancy can be overwhelming or reveal fears about becoming a mom. Later in this booklet, we will continue this topic, discussing feelings of guilt if you believe you contributed to the loss of the pregnancy.

Throughout all of your spiritual, physical, and emotional responses to your loss, you are not alone.

God understands it all, and He is with you, even when you feel confused. He loves you and will help you on this journey of grief.

A NOTE ON TRIGGERS

Your pain may be fresh. You recently lost your baby, and the memories of loss, bleeding, and grief are raw. You are still living the nightmare. Or maybe your pregnancy or infant loss was many years ago. Your wounds seem to have healed, yet at the most unpredictable times, grief hits you in your gut and leaves you breathless. Especially if you never processed through your loss, your grief may have been lingering under the surface for years, unresolved.

Given the nature of this booklet, you will likely be reminded of painful memories or hurtful conversations as you read. You may feel triggered, and old hurts may suddenly feel fresh. But if you have experienced a pregnancy or infant loss, this booklet is likely not your only trigger. You probably feel triggered on a regular basis. You feel triggered when you open your social media and see a new pregnancy announcement. You feel triggered when your friends ask you, "Are you pregnant yet?" or when a child yells, "Mom!" at church. You feel triggered when a mom complains about her many children, while you so desperately long for just one. You feel triggered each Mother's Day, Christmas, and back-to-school day, each occasion a painful reminder of your loss and what could have been.

Although it can be tempting, don't ignore your pain or race through this booklet. The balm of Scripture reaches into our moments of pain, and God joins us in our tears. He does not rush you in your grief. He does not discount your pain because "the pregnancy was early," as some of your friends may be tempted to do. God is patient and gentle. He values each life, and He mourns with you. Give yourself time to grieve your losses. Take the time to cry, journal, and pray. True healing comes from acknowledging our emotions, bringing them to the Lord, and finding hope in Him. Although the process of grief is painful, God has a purpose in it. Though it may feel impossible, He will use every pain, hurt, and disappointment for His glory and for your good.

A Prayer for the Hurting

My soul hurts. My eyes are red and worn out from crying. My body aches, and my heart hurts. I've never known pain like this. After losing my baby, my dreams and desires for the future also died. It's hard to have hope for tomorrow. Yet, even through death, I know that You are still God, and You are still good. You are still my heavenly Father, even when I can't see You or feel You. You hold all my tomorrows in Your hands, and nothing surprises You. You are my healer, comforter, and friend. At the same time, my faith feels weak. I don't know how I will go on. Would You comfort me? Would You help me draw near to You rather than pull away? In this season of grief, help me come to You, and please heal my hurting soul.

In Your good name,

Amen.

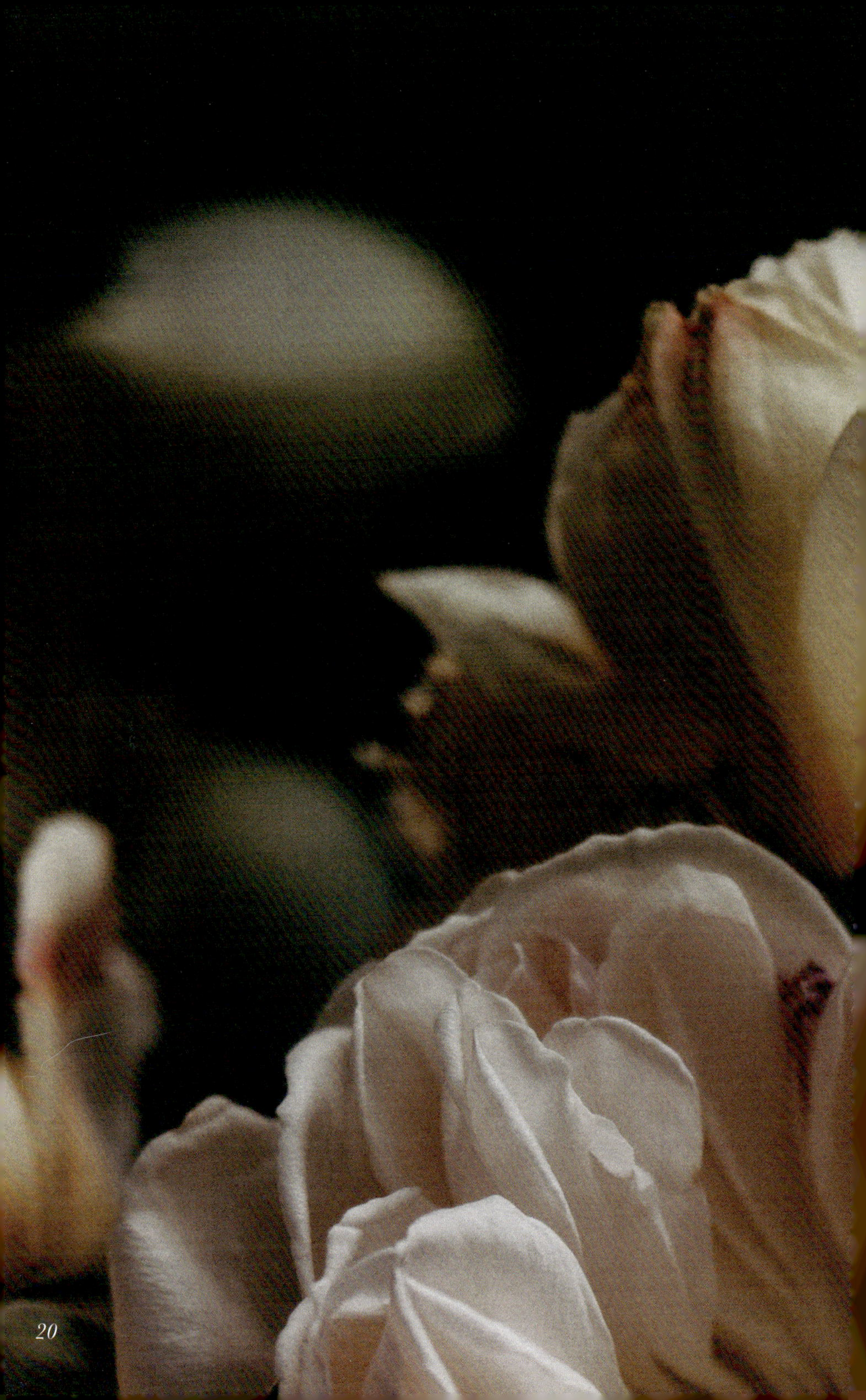

The balm of Scripture reaches into our moments of pain, and God joins us in our tears.

02.

Hope for Today

GOD IS WITH YOU

GOD WILL HELP YOU

GOD WILL MAKE
ALL THINGS RIGHT

GOD IS WITH YOU

Pregnancy and infant loss can be isolating forms of grief. A baby was alive in your belly. As much as others try to understand, relate, or empathize, they didn't feel what you felt. Sometimes well-meaning friends try to encourage you with trite, unhelpful sayings like, "At least you know you can get pregnant," while others seemingly ignore your pain. Throughout a pregnancy or infant loss, all of these factors compile like heavy stones weighing down your weary heart and making it easy to feel like no one understands. Yet, while it's normal to feel alone in our grief, the truth is that we are never alone.

We are never alone — even in the moments of our deepest shock, loss, and sorrow — because God is with us.

God has always been with you. He was with you through the initial loss, tears, and grief. He was with you through fertility tests and doctor's visits, through the fears, cramps, and treatments. When you saw the quiet, anxious look of your doctor as he stepped out of the room, leaving you by yourself, God was with you. When you were alone, crying and dizzy, and as blood rushed out of you with what seemed like no limit, He was there. When you were curled up in the fetal position on the cold bathroom floor in the middle of the night, He was there. He was with you then, and He is with you now. He is with you in the middle of the night when you can't sleep. He is with you when you dream of adding another stocking to your mantle at Christmastime. He is with you when your heart aches and when you feel numb. He is with you, and He understands. God, who is the source of all comfort, cries with you and grieves with you. He will never abandon you, no matter how sad, angry, or discouraged you feel. He will comfort you, and He will heal your broken heart.

God is not only with you—He was with your baby too.

Each life is invaluable, unique, and beautiful. Every life is known intimately by our Creator.

He cherished the life of your baby and carefully designed her in the womb. He formed her in His image and beheld her every heartbeat. He carefully guarded your baby from her conception and was with her every second. Just as you were never alone, neither was she.

GOD WILL HELP YOU

God will help you. He will help you through every test and medical decision. He will help you through every physical pain, emotional conversation, and unfulfilled longing. Through the hormones and night sweats, mental fog and blood loss, He cries with you and sustains you. He brings wisdom, comfort, and grace for each day. He will sustain you, whether this was the first baby you lost or if you've endured recurrent losses. He is your help.

God does not love us from afar, indifferently stiff-arming us or holding up His nose to our pain. Instead, He comes near. When Jesus was born on earth, He left the splendors of heaven to take on human flesh. He entered into our pain and experienced everyday human life. He was hungry, thirsty, and tired. He lost loved ones and endured pain, sorrow, and torture. He

Hope for Today

was condemned, slandered, betrayed by those closest to Him. He was crucified by those He loved. He died for the sins of people who were His enemies, and He rose from the dead to offer new life to all who would trust in Him. Jesus is called the "man of sorrows" because He knows what it means to grieve. He understands the depths of our emotions, and He can help you.

The mighty God of the universe has come near to us. He understands. He will help.

God is not like an insensitive doctor, pushing you to make medical decisions without time to grieve and reflect. He is not like a reserved ultrasound tech who stares at you with a blank face after doing a life-changing sonogram. He is near. He is compassionate and has all the power to help. He sees all, knows all, and has power over all. He will heal your heart and give you hope for tomorrow. And He will use every second of your pain for good. He will not waste a moment of your suffering, and He will help you get through today.

God does not love us from afar, indifferently stiff-arming us or holding up His nose to our pain.

Psalm 46:1-11

Read the words of Psalm 46, where the psalmist talked about God's help. Even through difficult and scary events—such as an earthquake, a war, or the mountains being thrown into the sea—the psalmist trusted in God as his safety and strength. He knew that God was his helper in times of trouble. He trusted that God was his refuge and strength. He didn't need to fear—not because his life was perfect but because God was with him. This doesn't mean that the psalmist was never anxious, angry, or discouraged. Rather, through the difficult times, he fixed his mind on what is true and found hope in the strength, protection, and help of God.

God is our refuge and strength,
a helper who is always found
in times of trouble.
Therefore we will not be afraid,
though the earth trembles
and the mountains topple
into the depths of the seas,
though its water roars and foams
and the mountains quake with its turmoil.   *Selah*

There is a river—
its streams delight the city of God,
the holy dwelling place of the Most High.
God is within her; she will not be toppled.
God will help her when the morning dawns.

Nations rage, kingdoms topple;
the earth melts when he lifts his voice.
The Lord of Armies is with us;
the God of Jacob is our stronghold.   *Selah*

Come, see the works of the Lord,
who brings devastation on the earth.
He makes wars cease throughout the earth.
He shatters bows and cuts spears to pieces;
he sets wagons ablaze.
"Stop fighting, and know that I am God,
exalted among the nations, exalted on the earth."
The Lord of Armies is with us;
the God of Jacob is our stronghold.   *Selah*

After you read Psalm 46, write your own prayer to the Lord inspired by Psalm 46.

Here is an example:

God, You are my refuge and strength. Even when I lost my baby, even when my body is hurting and my heart is anxious, I don't need to be afraid because You are with me. You are my help, even when I can't see You. Even when I can't understand why You've allowed these things to happen, You are still good. You promise in the Bible that You will help me each day. Will You please help? I'm still afraid, hurting, and broken, but I'm trying to trust You. Help me trust You.

Pray Psalm 46

32

Jesus is called the "man of sorrows" because He knows what it means to grieve.

Sometimes, miscarriages or stillbirths give us warning signs: irregular spotting or measuring small on ultrasounds. Maybe you were told to be "cautiously optimistic" by your doctor because of concerning medical results. You felt torn between careful optimism and excitedly dreaming about a future life with your child. But sometimes, this loss comes without warning, like a truck running bullishly through a red light and crashing recklessly into oncoming traffic. There was no warning of the incoming destruction. It was not invited, but now, there is only devastation left in its wake. It feels like evil has entered into the safety of your womb without your permission, leaving you with no power to protect the little one in your care.

The loss of a child can make us feel powerless. It reminds us that we are not in control. But although we can feel powerless in our grief, God is always in control, and He promises to make all things right. His character is good, and He is just. One day, He will come again to restore every broken thing. There will be no more sorrow or grief, no more unfulfilled desires or desperate longings. There will be no more empty cribs or returned registry items. There will be no more death. God is a God of peace, wholeness, and life.

When Jesus returns, He will right every wrong and restore every broken thing.

He will remove every sickness, every pain, and every sorrow (Revelation 21:4). He will wipe every tear from our eyes and heal every hurt. He will make all things new.

Revelation 21:1–6

Then I saw a new heaven and a new earth; for the first heaven and the first earth had passed away, and the sea was no more. I also saw the holy city, the new Jerusalem, coming down out of heaven from God, prepared like a bride adorned for her husband.

Then I heard a loud voice from the throne: Look, God's dwelling is with humanity, and he will live with them. They will be his peoples, and God himself will be with them and will be their God. He will wipe away every tear from their eyes. Death will be no more; grief, crying, and pain will be no more, because the previous things have passed away.

Then the one seated on the throne said, "Look, I am making everything new." He also said, "Write, because these words are faithful and true." Then he said to me, "It is done! I am the Alpha and the Omega, the beginning and the end. I will freely give to the thirsty from the spring of the water of life.

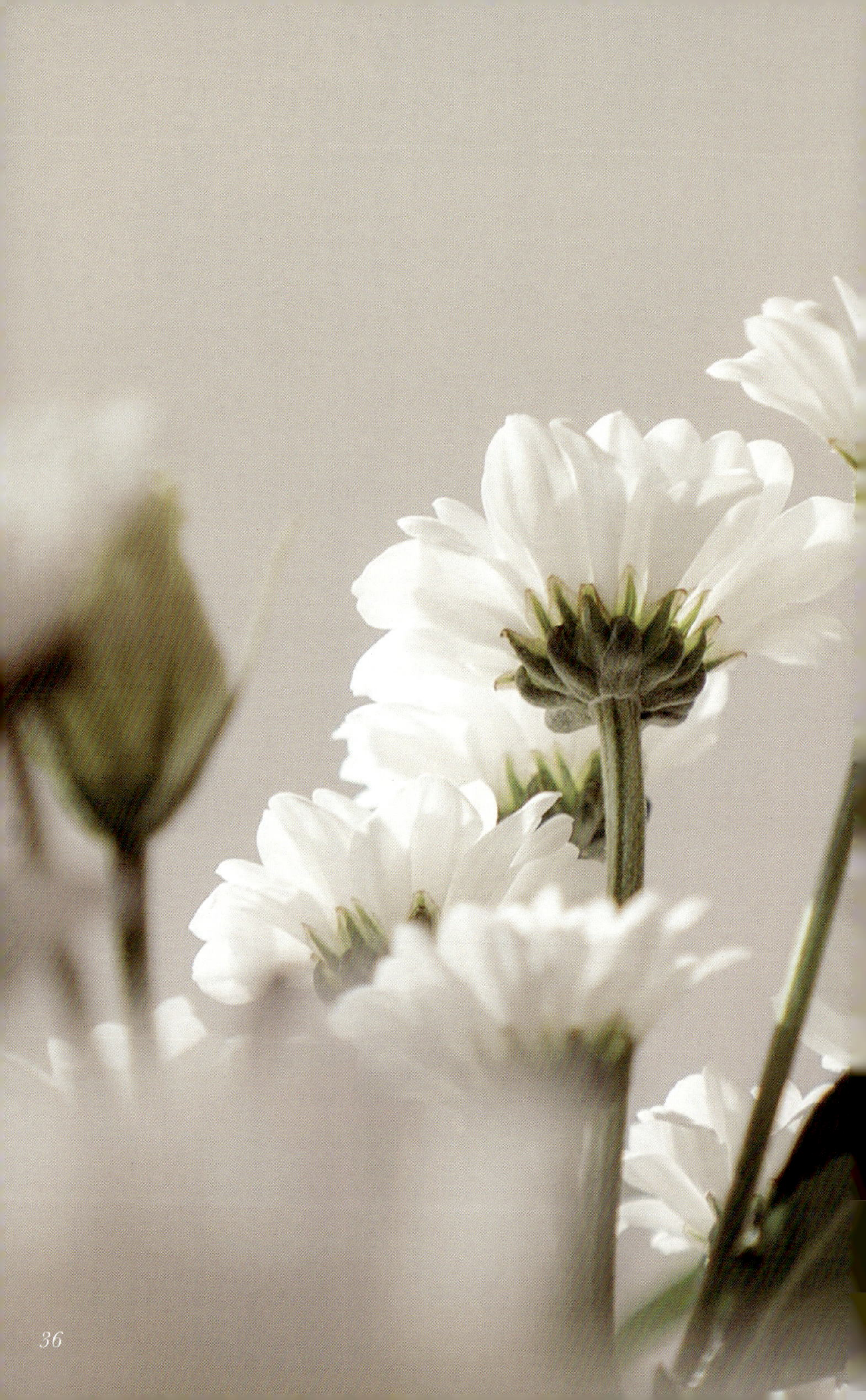

God is always in control, and He promises to make all things right.

03.
Mourning Your Loss

BIBLICAL LAMENT

BE HONEST WITH
YOUR EMOTIONS

HONESTLY EVALUATE
FEELINGS OF GUILT

UNDERSTAND YOUR
IDENTITY IN CHRIST

BIBLICAL COMMUNITY

WHEN GOD SAYS NO:
TRUSTING GOD IN SUFFERING

FIND HOPE IN SCRIPTURE

PLANNING A CEREMONY
TO GRIEVE THE LOSS

HAVE A PLAN FOR
IMPORTANT DATES

BIBLICAL LAMENT

Biblical lament is crying out to God in our grief, sorrow, or loss. The Bible is full of passages filled with men and women who cried out to the Lord through their difficult emotions. Hannah, for example, desperately cried out to the Lord in her season of barrenness. Through her longings, distress, and sadness, she prayed to the Lord for a child and brought all her desires to Him. In fact, she cried out to God with such emotion that a watching priest thought she was drunk (1 Samuel 1:10–17). Hannah's pleas are joined in Scripture by the words of the psalmists, who cried out to the Lord in depression, anger, sadness, and despair. They were raw and honest before the Lord, not hiding their emotions from God but bringing everything to Him. We, too, should bring all of our emotions to the Lord.

God is not surprised by our feelings. He is the Creator of emotions, and He is our help in processing them.

He has heard the prayer, cry, and longing of every person throughout history, and He has the power to help us too.

When we are anxious, angry, or sad, we often instinctively withdraw from God. We want to close ourselves off emotionally to hold off the pain. But God offers us something better. He invites us to find peace as we talk to Him about all of our fears (Philippians 4:6–7). He invites us to come to Him with all our emotions. We can press into Him to find comfort, hope, and life. We can come to Him in rage, exhaustion, anger, and sadness. We can pour all of our emotions out to the Lord, knowing that He will comfort us.

We can pour all of our emotions out to the Lord, knowing that He will comfort us.

Identifying Your Emotions

Use this page to identify how you're feeling.
Then express your thoughts, emotions, and fears
to the Lord through prayer.

Circle any emotions you're currently feeling:

Sadness	Hopelessness
Anger	Envy
Despair	Loneliness
Shock	Guilt
Fear	Anger
Depression	Peace
Confusion	Emptiness
Relief	Other _____

List the emotions you circled. Then, tell the Lord
how you're feeling, and ask for His help.

BE HONEST WITH YOUR EMOTIONS

Maybe you don't know how to process what you're feeling. You've stuffed your emotions deep down, pushing them to the side so that you can show up in everyday life. You've compartmentalized your pregnancy or infant loss, not wanting to process your loss. Or maybe you didn't have a chance to dream about the future before you started spotting. The loss feels disorienting, like a rapid rollercoaster from joy to grief, and all you know is that it hurts. It hurts to be around those with babies or children. It hurts to see beautiful flowers because they remind you of death. It hurts to think about what could have been. Your emotions feel volatile and unpredictable. One moment you feel jealous and angry at the plethora of pregnancy and birth announcements, and a moment later, you feel numb.

An important part of healing is being honest with your emotions. This includes naming them and finding God's comfort for every emotion. One helpful way to do this is through journaling. Write down your thoughts, emotions, and prayers. Find creative expressions for your grief, such as through painting, drawing, or playing music. Name your emotions as you experience them, from shock and denial to anger and depression. Find a trusted friend, and share how you're feeling. Talk about the "what-ifs," the disappointments, the dreams unfulfilled, and the desires postponed.

As you identify your emotions, be compassionate with yourself, and give yourself time to grieve. The loss of a baby is not something to just "get over." It will take time to identify your emotions and journal through them. Take time to cry, and be honest with those around you. It's okay to not be okay. One day, God will bring comfort to your grieving heart. Until then, find hope that God is with you and cares for the brokenhearted.

For more biblical help on emotions, check out the *Emotions and the Heart* study or the *Gospel Hope in Grief and Loss* booklet from The Daily Grace Co.

Use this journaling space to process your story, thoughts, and emotions:

The Bible presents a better, truer narrative than our condemning self-judgments; it offers hope and peace.

HONESTLY EVALUATE FEELINGS OF GUILT

Guilt is the dark, hidden secret of many women who experience pregnancy or infant loss. Guilt can take on many forms, from anxiety to anger. It often evades logic and dwells in darkness like a slithering, slippery snake. It plunges its victims into depression and taunts them with condemning questions, leaving remorse, embarrassment, and shame in its wake.

Perhaps you feel guilty for your pregnancy or infant loss because of something you did. You wonder if you miscarried because you had a glass of wine or because you continued your birth control pills before knowing you were pregnant. You wonder, *Did I exercise too much? Was I too fearful about the pregnancy? Should I have laid my baby on her back, not her stomach? Is God punishing me for something I did in my past?*

Or maybe you feel guilty after your miscarriage or infant loss because of something you didn't do. Maybe you feel guilty because you didn't know you were miscarrying. You carried the baby for several weeks before finding out about the miscarriage on an ultrasound. You hear the voice of condemnation saying, *Aren't women supposed to have a sixth sense about these kinds of things? Why couldn't I sense the loss of life inside me?* Or maybe you feel plagued by the thought that if only you had gotten more rest, taken prenatal vitamins, or seen a doctor sooner, your baby would still be alive.

Questions of guilt often swirl around our minds as we try to find a reason for our pain. Sometimes, it is easier to blame ourselves for a loss than to recognize that we are not in control. But—in truth—death, disease, miscarriage, stillbirth, and infant loss are the devastating effects of living in a broken world. The Bible presents a better, truer narrative than our condemning self-judgments; it offers hope and peace. If you are a Christian, there is no longer any shame or condemnation for you in Christ.

Jesus has taken guilt and shame, and He has removed their power through the cross. He has paid for our guilt and shame once and for all through His perfect sacrifice so that we don't need to carry them anymore. God does not condemn you but sees you as spotless because of Jesus's righteousness. If you feel burdened with guilt and shame, bring your thoughts to the light. Express your feelings of guilt to the Lord in prayer and repentance, write about them in a journal, and talk about them with a trusted friend. Read the verses on the next page, and find comfort in the love and freedom offered to you in Christ. Remember that God is gracious and covers over our guilt and condemnation through His Son.

As you are processing feelings of guilt, you may also discover residual feelings of shame, as if something is wrong with you. You may feel shame because you wish your story had turned out differently or because your body seemed to fail you. You may feel shame for questioning God's goodness and faithfulness. But regardless of this guilt or shame we may feel, we can press into the Lord and pour out our hearts to Him, telling Him about all of our hopes, fears, and unfulfilled longings.

Although we do not know why God allows certain hardships in our lives, we trust that He is still good, and He can comfort our hearts even through deep disappointment.

Even when it feels like your body has betrayed you, God has not abandoned you.

He is not ashamed of you. He does not think less of you, and He will use even this trauma for your good.

Because of the gospel, we can find hope through our sorrow.

He is in control, and He is good, though the circumstances around us don't feel good. God is gracious, patient, and long-suffering. He is sovereign over every detail of our lives. He will use every loss for good.

Freedom in Christ Verses

Therefore, there is now no condemnation for those in Christ Jesus, because the law of the Spirit of life in Christ Jesus has set you free from the law of sin and death.

ROMANS 8:1–2

If we confess our sins, he is faithful and righteous to forgive us our sins and to cleanse us from all unrighteousness.

1 JOHN 1:9

For God did not send his Son into the world to condemn the world, but to save the world through him.

JOHN 3:17

Dear friends, if our hearts don't condemn us, we have confidence before God and receive whatever we ask from him because we keep his commands and do what is pleasing in his sight. Now this is his command: that we believe in the name of his Son, Jesus Christ, and love one another as he commanded us. The one who keeps his commands remains in him, and he in him. And the way we know that he remains in us is from the Spirit he has given us.

1 JOHN 3:21–24

UNDERSTAND YOUR IDENTITY IN CHRIST

"Congratulations, you're a mom!" When you found out you were pregnant with your first child, your entire identity changed. Maybe your old titles of employee, daughter, or wife seemed to momentarily dull as you tried on your sparkling new name, "Mom." You imagined your baby's first word being an adorable, babbling, and toothless, "Mama." You felt an unimaginable maternal love grow within you and knew that there wasn't anything you wouldn't do for your baby.

In an instant, you made plans for the future. You had ambitions about the kind of mom you'd be: patient and kind, healthy yet flexible. You read books and started dreaming about your new life, from kissing tiny toes and little eyelashes to changing diapers and nursing. You made plans for the holidays with visions of Christmas cookies, books before the fire, and puffy pink snowsuits. You wondered about your child's future with hope. What sports would your child enjoy? Would she play an instrument? Would he like to hunt?

As your plans grew, your body grew, too. Perhaps your body started to experience pregnancy symptoms, food aversions, nausea, and exhaustion. Maybe you even started to show or feel little baby kicks in the night. Until suddenly, the loss of your baby abolished your dreams. You felt the void, not only within your womb but also within your visions for the future. Would Christmas ever hold the joyful memories you envisioned? Would anyone ever call you mom? If you were able to hold your baby, you relive each moment you had with him or her. Joy mixes with sorrow as you recall his little toes and eyelashes, fingers and nose.

After loss, our identity changes. The grief of death produces pain, not only in the present but also in its disappointments for the future. Yet, even through our pain, God has not abandoned us. He is with us in our grief and comforts us in it. He has given us an eternal hope and unchanging purpose as His children. He has called us His beloved daughters, chosen and precious to Him. He cares for us.

One of the ways God cares for us is through our new identities in the gospel. When God saved us, He gave us a calling that never changes. He made us His heirs, saints, beloved, forgiven, and set free.

We're known and loved, God's masterpieces who are beautifully and wonderfully made.

The joy of being a child of God does not remove the pain of pregnancy and infant loss, but it does reorient our hope. Even if you don't have a child who calls you "Mom," you are not "lesser than" as a woman. Your primary purpose in life remains: to know God and enjoy Him forever. God has beautiful plans for you, and His grace is sufficient, even when our other life titles change. The joy of being a child of God, loved by your Maker and on mission for Him, will never fade.

Through grief, we must cling to the One who will never disappoint, fade, or change.

Mourning Your Loss

Identity in Christ

Read the following verses, and underline characteristics of your identity in Christ:

Therefore, if anyone is in Christ, he is a new creation; the old has passed away, and see, the new has come! Everything is from God, who has reconciled us to himself through Christ and has given us the ministry of reconciliation. That is, in Christ, God was reconciling the world to himself, not counting their trespasses against them, and he has committed the message of reconciliation to us. Therefore, we are ambassadors for Christ, since God is making his appeal through us. We plead on Christ's behalf, "Be reconciled to God." He made the one who did not know sin to be sin for us, so that in him we might become the righteousness of God.

2 CORINTHIANS 5:17–21

So if you have been raised with Christ, seek the things above, where Christ is, seated at the right hand of God. Set your minds on things above, not on earthly things. For you died, and your life is hidden with Christ in God. When Christ, who is your life, appears, then you also will appear with him in glory.

COLOSSIANS 3:1–4

Our citizenship is in heaven, and we eagerly wait for a Savior from there, the Lord Jesus Christ. He will transform the body of our humble condition into the likeness of his glorious body, by the power that enables him to subject everything to himself.

PHILIPPIANS 3:20–21

But you are a chosen race, a royal priesthood, a holy nation, a people for his possession, so that you may proclaim the praises of the one who called you out of darkness into his marvelous light. Once you were not a people, but now you are God's people; you had not received mercy, but now you have received mercy.

1 PETER 2:9–10

BIBLICAL COMMUNITY

We were never meant to do life on our own. We all need a family to walk through life with us, especially in seasons of loss. We need brothers and sisters who will pray for us, encourage us, and remind us of the faithful love of God. We need friends with strong faith in seasons when we feel like we're drowning. We need pastors who will care for our broken hearts and pray for us when we're weak. Thankfully, God has given us a family through the local church.

Although it is tempting to withdraw from others after the loss of a child, try to show up. Press into community, even when it's hard. Go to church on Sunday, even if you feel the need to wear sunglasses to cover the bags under your eyes. Identify two or three trusted friends with whom you can confide your deepest thoughts and emotions. You do not need to share your deepest emotions with everyone. Rather, find a few women who will not gossip and who will encourage you in God's Word as you share your thoughts, hopes, dreams, and disappointments with them.

Over time, you will discover that God has started to bind your wounds and heal your hurts. As He does, look for women you can support, love, and encourage. God has comforted you so that you can comfort others. Your suffering will never be wasted, and you too will be able to encourage hurting brothers and sisters through their losses.

Not only this, but if you experienced a pregnancy or infant loss and currently have no children at home, you can still be a spiritual mother within the Church. You can have a divine, God-ordained, important role as an older woman mentoring younger girls. You can love, provide wisdom, and encourage younger women in your local church. Titus 2:3-5 tells us:

> In the same way, older women are to be reverent in behavior, not slanderers, not slaves to excessive drinking. They are to teach what is good, so that they may encourage the young women to love their husbands and to love their children, to be self-controlled, pure, workers at home, kind, and in submission to their husbands, so that God's word will not be slandered.

Discipling does not replace the role of a child in your life, but it can help provide purpose in a confusing season. After you have taken time to grieve, find a woman who is younger than you, and begin to pour into her. If you would like to disciple another woman but are unsure how to start, the *Better Together* discipleship study from The Daily Grace Co. may be a great resource for you to use.

We need the Church and biblical community, both to be served and to serve.

When we are members of Bible-believing churches, we do not need to face our trials alone. Our brothers and sisters hold up our faith when we cannot stand on our own. And one day, perhaps we will be able to help someone do the same.

Wellness Checklist

Grief affects every area of our lives. It not only alters our emotions, but it also takes a big toll on our bodies.

After losing a baby, you may notice that your body is greatly fatigued, stressed, and exhausted. You may feel forgetful, have trouble sleeping, or have a hard time concentrating. Your body may feel burdened with backaches, headaches, and sickness. Ordinary tasks, such as cooking dinner or doing laundry, seem like insurmountable hurdles. This is normal. Especially in the midst of a physically stressful time, it is important to create regular rhythms to take care of your body.

If you find it difficult to remember daily tasks, consider creating your own checklist to maintain normal rhythms of health. This list may include:

- [ ] TALK TO GOD, AND READ HIS WORD
- [ ] TAKE VITAMINS
- [ ] GO FOR A WALK OUTSIDE
- [ ] SIT OUTSIDE IN THE SUNLIGHT
- [ ] DRINK WATER
- [ ] EAT REGULAR, HEALTHY MEALS
- [ ] CALL A FRIEND
- [ ] _____
- [ ] _____

Your suffering will never be wasted.

WHEN GOD SAYS NO: TRUSTING GOD IN SUFFERING

One of the most difficult aspects of a pregnancy or infant loss is disappointment. For a season, God said "no" to your dreams. Fear of a barren future mingles with disappointment in the present. The emotional pain of dreams deferred trumps even the unbearable physical pain of the loss itself. You may even recall with heavy pain the delight you once had in changing and feeding your baby, but now, it's all over.

Even still, we can trust God in our suffering. Throughout Scripture, men and women often faced disappointing circumstances, from the loss of loved ones to exile from their homeland. They endured unspeakable grief and pain and learned to trust God, even when life hurts. Read the words that Habakkuk wrote in the midst of an invasion from the Babylonians and very real uncertainty about tomorrow:

> Though the fig tree does not bud and there is no fruit on the vines, though the olive crop fails and the fields produce no food, though the flocks disappear from the pen and there are no herds in the stalls, yet I will celebrate in the Lord; I will rejoice in the God of my salvation! The Lord my Lord is my strength; he makes my feet like those of a deer and enables me to walk on mountain heights! (Habakkuk 3:17–19)

Habakkuk was able to rejoice in God because he knew that God was his ultimate treasure. Though the world around us will fail, God remains secure. He is the hope, joy, and peace our soul craves. He is greater than babies, diapers, and butterfly kisses. He is our hope, greater than school pictures, play dates, and sticky mac 'n cheese fingers. While it is not wrong to long for children—indeed, they are a blessing—we must also remember that we have everything we need in Christ. Even when God says "no" or "not yet" to your good desire for kids, He is still good. We can pour out our hearts to Him in prayer, asking for these desires, and we can rest, knowing that He is good and holds the universe in His hands.

Psalm 23

The Lord is my shepherd;

I have what I need.

He lets me lie down in green pastures;

he leads me beside quiet waters.

He renews my life;

he leads me along the right paths

for his name's sake.

Even when I go through the darkest valley,

I fear no danger,

for you are with me;

your rod and your staff — they comfort me.

You prepare a table before me

in the presence of my enemies;

you anoint my head with oil;

my cup overflows.

Only goodness and faithful love will pursue me

all the days of my life,

and I will dwell in the house of the Lord

as long as I live.

FIND HOPE IN SCRIPTURE

When our world feels like it's crumbling, we need a sure foundation. Thankfully, God has not left us alone. He has given us His Spirit to dwell within us and His Word as a lamp to our feet. Both His Spirit and His Word remind us what is true when we feel like we're blindly groping in the dark. They are our confidence, encouragement, and hope in every season. They are our help and our shield.

Consider what Scripture says about suffering, for example. Instead of condemning us for our grief, Jesus calls us to come to Him for rest. He says, "Come to me, all of you who are weary and burdened, and I will give you rest. Take up my yoke and learn from me, because I am lowly and humble in heart, and you will find rest for your souls" (Matthew 11:28–29). In His Word, God promises that He will use all our pain for our good and His glory (Romans 8:28). Miraculously, the Bible also calls us to do something difficult: to consider it joy when we endure various trials (James 1:2). He says that those who mourn are blessed, for they will be comforted (Matthew 5:4). In God's economy, God reverses the pain of death and uses every sorrow for good.

Scripture is our safety when the world around us feels unstable.

It is our foundation, an unchanging truth, and our present hope. When you are angry, turn to God's Word. When you can't find hope for the future, find hope in Scripture. When you fear tomorrow or are bitter at all the birth announcements around you, turn to the words of Scripture to find encouragement and help.

Lamentations 3:17–26

I have been deprived of peace;
I have forgotten what prosperity is.
Then I thought, "My future is lost,
as well as my hope from the Lord."

Remember my affliction and my homelessness,
the wormwood and the poison.
I continually remember them
and have become depressed.
Yet I call this to mind,
and therefore I have hope:

Because of the Lord's faithful love
we do not perish,
for his mercies never end.
They are new every morning;
great is your faithfulness!
I say, "The Lord is my portion,
therefore I will put my hope in him."

The Lord is good to those who wait for him,
to the person who seeks him.
It is good to wait quietly
for salvation from the Lord.

Have grace with yourself, and don't expect life to immediately revert to normal — give yourself permission to grieve.

PLANNING A CEREMONY TO GRIEVE THE LOSS

Many women don't take time off after a miscarriage. They go back to work immediately, blocking out memories of ultrasounds and hCG tests, mood swings, lower back pain, blood, and contractions. Even if they desire to slow down and grieve, life's responsibilities continue to flood in and bearishly stunt the grieving process.

If you are able, take bereavement time from work after your pregnancy or infant loss so that you can mourn. Even if this is not possible at your workplace, have grace with yourself, and don't expect life to immediately revert to normal—give yourself permission to grieve. The loss of a baby to miscarriage or stillbirth is still the loss of a child.

Take time to cry and mourn the brokenness of the world.

For some parents, planning a funeral can be a beautiful way to honor their baby's life. Even if you were not able to physically hold your baby, you can still plan a ceremony or celebration of life for your child. Choose a select few to invite, read a few chosen Scriptures, ask for prayer over your family, and remember your baby with others. Or maybe you prefer a more private way to remember your baby. You could prayerfully choose a necklace that reminds you of your baby every time you wear it. Or you could create a memory box or scrapbook to compile ultrasound pictures, positive pregnancy tests, or baby outfits.

Remembering Your Baby

*Use these pages to brainstorm how you would
like to honor the life of your baby:*

What would you like to do to celebrate the life of your baby? Would you like a public or private ceremony?

_____

_____

_____

_____

Is there a physical item, verse, or poem that you would like to choose to remember your baby?

_____

_____

_____

_____

If you want to hold a celebration of life event, what is your vision for a ceremony?

_____

_____

_____

_____

_____

_____

Who would you like to invite?

_____

_____

_____

_____

Where would you like the ceremony to take place?

_____

_____

_____

_____

When would you like to hold the celebration of life?

_____

_____

_____

_____

What elements would you like to include during the celebration (Scripture reading, family speaking, etc.)?

_____

_____

_____

How would you like to remember your baby during future holidays? (Ideas may include buying a stocking for Christmas, planting a tree in your yard, asking your husband to buy you flowers for Mother's Day, etc.)

_____

_____

_____

Other ideas:

_____

_____

_____

_____

_____

_____

_____

_____

_____

_____

Because of the Lord's faithful love we do not perish, for his mercies never end.

— LAMENTATIONS 3:22

HAVE A PLAN FOR IMPORTANT DATES

Certain days are hard for mamas who have experienced pregnancy or infant loss. Mother's Day, Father's Day, back-to-school season, and Christmas celebrations often stir up fresh grief and pain. You watch moms around you tiredly complain about how they want a break for Mother's Day, and all you can think about is how you long for a baby who would make you tired. It's especially easy to feel robbed of blessings on holidays and anniversaries. Everywhere you look, women seem to be pregnant. Your heart aches at the newest baby announcements as you grieve what would have been your due date.

If you know a difficult day is coming, make a plan for that day in advance. Decide what you will do for the day and who you will spend time with. Take a break from social media if needed, or plan a special outing. If your difficult days are also communal days such as Mother's Day, look for other women who are hurting because of the loss of their child or mothers. As you grieve, remember also to take care of your body. Get proper rest, take your vitamins, and protect your mind with what technology you consume.

One day, life will not be so hard. Your grief will lessen, and you will be able to celebrate the life of your baby rather than mourn his or her loss. Until that day comes, find hope that God is your comfort and strength.

God will help you get through each day, even these intensely triggering ones.

Make a Plan

Make a plan for difficult days by working through the following questions:

What days or times are particularly difficult days of grief?

_____

_____

_____

What specific aspects, conversations, or triggers make those days difficult?

_____

_____

_____

Make a plan for each day. Think about who you'd like to spend the day with, where you'd like to go, and what you'd like to do.

_____

_____

_____

_____

_____

_____

_____

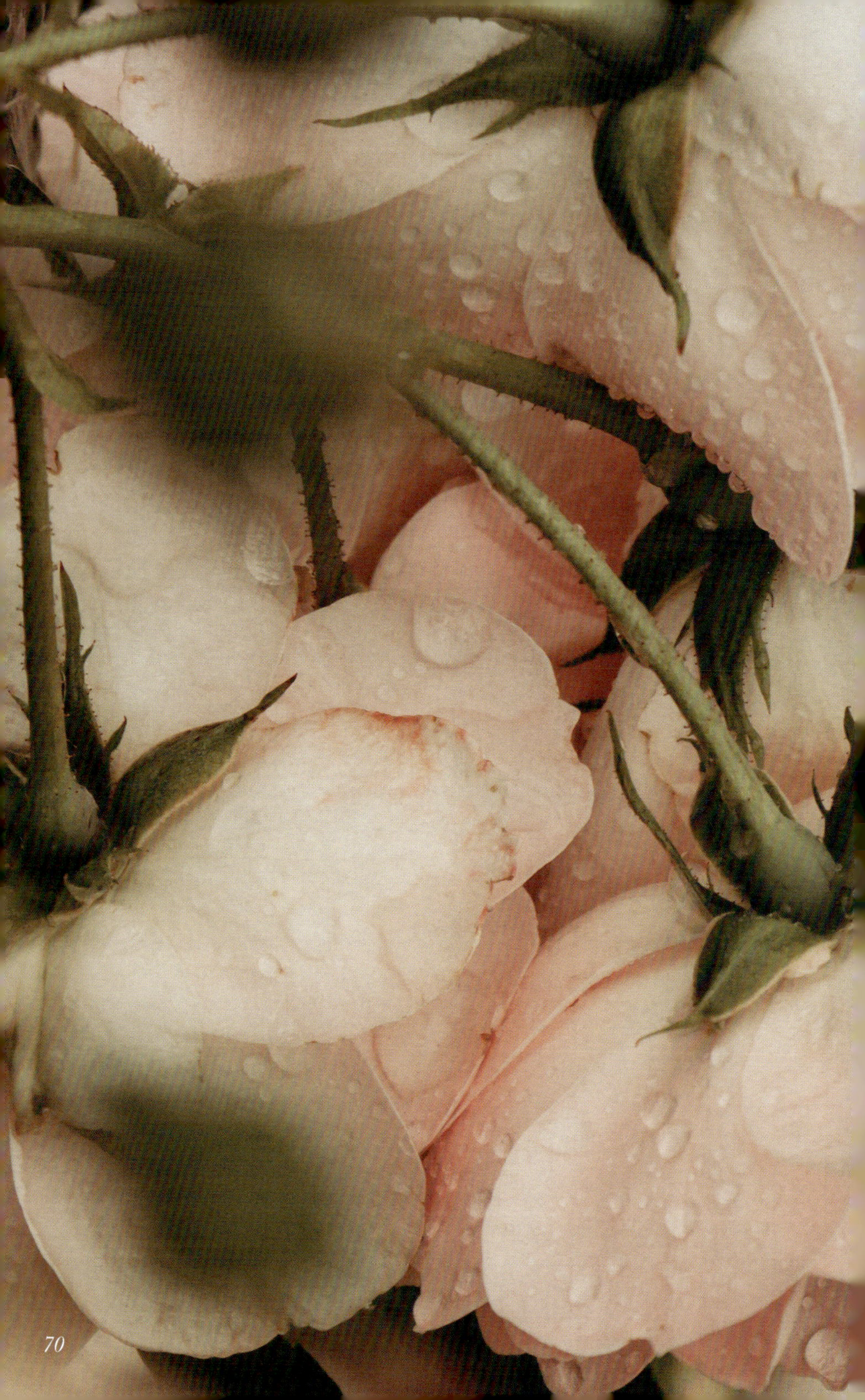

*Truly, God understands
the pain of losing a child.*

04.
Common Questions

WHERE IS GOD?

IS GOD PUNISHING ME?

WHY DID GOD ALLOW THIS
TO HAPPEN TO ME?

WAS MY UNBORN BABY
A REAL PERSON?

WHERE IS MY BABY NOW?

WILL THIS HAPPEN AGAIN?

WILL THE PAIN EVER END?

WHERE IS GOD?

After a pregnancy or infant loss, it is easy to feel alone. You may wonder, *Where was God when I was dizzy from blood loss and night sweats? Where was He in the cramping, mental fog, despair, and pain? If He is good and if He is real, why would He allow my baby to die?* But the truth is this: you were never alone. The God of the universe has always been with you, caring for you and protecting you. God was with you when you found out you were pregnant, and He was with you in the doctor's office when you heard the news of no heartbeat. He was with your baby, loving her, as she passed from this life to the next. He was with you, guiding you when you were making decisions to have a D&C or let the baby pass naturally. He has been with you throughout your entire pregnancy, miscarriage, stillbirth, or infant loss, and He remains with you throughout the grieving process. God has been with you the whole time—holding you, protecting you, and caring for you. You were never alone.

Although God may feel distant in our grief, Scripture reminds us that He is near, and He understands our pain. Not only was God with you throughout your loss, but He knows firsthand what it feels like to lose a child. God is the perfect Father who passionately loves His Son. He lovingly delighted over Jesus while He was on earth, just as you joyfully cherished your child. He was there as Jesus dropped tears of blood and died a bloody, criminal death on a cross. He was there as His Son bore the weight of the shame of the world on His shoulders. God didn't stand emotionless through Jesus's gruesome death. He didn't hold back His love for an instant. Instead, His Father's love experienced the full grief of loss.

Truly, God understands the pain of losing a child.

He has always been with you. He knows what you are feeling, and He empathizes with your pain.

C. S. Lewis on Suffering and Grief

In C. S. Lewis's classic children's series *The Chronicles of Narnia*, there is a beautiful story of a little boy named Digory. His mother was sick, and he went to the lion to ask for healing. He said:

> "But please, please — won't you — can't you give me something that will cure Mother?' Up till then he had been looking at the Lion's great feet and the huge claws on them; now, in his despair, he looked up at its face. What he saw surprised him as much as anything in his whole life. For the tawny face was bent down near his own and (wonder of wonders) great shining tears stood in the Lion's eyes. They were such big, bright tears compared with Digory's own that for a moment he felt as if the Lion must really be sorrier about his Mother than he was himself.
>
> "My son, my son," said Aslan. "I know. Grief is great."

> *God has not abandoned you in your grief. Rather, He is crying with you.*

He will sustain you in your grief, and He will heal your broken heart.

IS GOD PUNISHING ME?

After a pregnancy or infant loss, it is easy to wonder why God allowed this tragedy to happen. You may wonder: *Did I do something to deserve it? Is God mad at me or punishing me for some past sexual sin?*

In the face of these questions, take heart. God is not punishing you, dear Christian. When we trust in Christ, we are forgiven of our sins and adopted as God's children. Because of the life, death, and resurrection of Jesus, we no longer need to fear God's judgment. His wrath and anger were fully absorbed on the cross, and if you are in Christ, you can be confident that there is no more condemnation for you (Romans 8:1). He is perfectly pleased with you because of Jesus.

While it is easy to imagine God as a condemning judge in the midst of our grief, theologically, we know that bad things happen to believers on earth, not as a sign of God's judgment or wrath but because of the fall (Genesis 1–3). When Adam and Eve disobeyed God, death was introduced into the world. Evil, sickness, and death invaded the safety of a good world. Now, we wrestle against aging bodies, infertility struggles, and pregnancy and infant losses. We lose those we love and endure unspeakable pain.

Thankfully, God does not abandon us, even in our deepest moments of grief. He cares for us and loves us, providing everything that we need. He helps us and delights in us, not because we've done anything to deserve it but because of His unchanging character. God allows us to experience hardship at times, not out of condemnation but as a loving Father who promises to use our suffering to grow our faith and refine us into His image (Romans 8:28, Hebrews 12:7–11, James 1:2–4). We were saved by grace. This should comfort our weary souls, even through the heavy swamps of grief. We weren't saved by anything we did, nor can we sustain God's favor by anything we do.

We are loved, saved, adopted, and redeemed solely by God's merciful, loving, and overwhelming grace.

If you continually feel ashamed because of your pregnancy or infant loss, remember: God is merciful. He is sympathetic toward your pain. He works through your weaknesses, and He uses the things that are weak to shame the strong (1 Corinthians 1:27). When grief feels dark and heavy, press into the ordinary means of grace. Dive into Scripture, meditate on the Psalms, and pour out your heart before the Lord. Listen to truth-filled music, and share your burdens with another brother or sister in Christ.

God will never abandon you in your moments of grief; He will carry you through them.

Although we live in bodies that are like fragile jars of clay, God promises to use even our weaknesses to display His mercy and grace.

DAVID POWLISON:
Our Sufferings and God's Grace

David Powlison was a biblical counselor who taught God's Word. He shared the hope of Scripture to a broken world and brought encouragement, comfort, and healing to many. Read what he says about suffering in his book *God's Grace in Your Suffering*:

> How will God actually engage *your* sufferings with his grace? You may know the right answer in theory. You may have known it firsthand in some difficult situations. And yet, you'll find that you don't know God well enough or in the exact ways you need to for the next thing that comes your way.
>
> We take God's hard answer and make it sound like a pat answer. He sets about a long slow answer*ing*, but we're after a quick fix. His answer insists on being lived out over time and into the particulars. We act as if just saying the right words makes it so. God's answer involves changing you into a different kind of person. But we act as if some truth, principle, strategy, or perspective might simply be incorporated into who we already are. God personalizes his answer on hearts with an uncanny flexibility. But we turn it into a formula: "If you just believe x. If you just do y. If you just remember z." No important truth even contains the word "just" in the punch line.
>
> We can make the right answer sound old hat, but I guarantee this: God will surprise you. He will make you stop. You will struggle. He will

bring you up short. You will hurt. He will take his time. You will grow in faith and in love. He will deeply delight you. You will find the process harder than you ever imagined—and better. Goodness and mercy will follow you all the days of your life. At the end of the long road you will come home at last. No matter how many times you've heard it, no matter how long you've known it, no matter how well you can say it, God's answer will come to mean something better than you could ever imagine.

He answers with himself.

WHY DID GOD ALLOW THIS TO HAPPEN TO ME?

Children are called a "blessing" or a "reward" in Scripture (Psalm 127:3), yet your body has been unable to sustain a pregnancy. You might wonder: *Am I cursed? Why would God allow this to happen?* Or perhaps you think about how many women experience unwanted pregnancies while you've remained faithful to the Lord and so desperately desire a child. You ache with questions like: *Why won't God bless me with the gift of motherhood when I've been true to Him? Why have I had to endure the loss of child after child when so many pregnant women didn't even want to get pregnant?*

Unfortunately, there is no easy or satisfying answer for why your pregnancy or infant loss happened. For many of life's trials, we do not understand why God allowed them to occur. Because of the fall, evil and tragedies plague our world, and sadly, this includes the loss of children through pregnancy and infant loss. While this theological truth remains, God offers us this hope: He will use this pain for His glory and your good. He will be with you in trouble, and He will make all things right.

Your suffering and pain are not meaningless.

God promises to use every loss to refine us and shape us into His image.

Though we may not understand why God allowed us to experience this specific grief, we know that He will use it for His everlasting, eternal purposes—to bring joy, peace, a longing for heaven, steadfastness, and faith. He will comfort you so that you can comfort others. He will refine you and strengthen your character. He will sustain you and satisfy your fragile heart with His goodness and love.

When we examine the whole narrative of Scripture, we discover that Christians are not promised a life free from trouble. The prophets, John the Baptist, and even Jesus Himself endured unspeakable pain and sorrow on this earth. In every case, God accomplished His purposes to sustain, purify, and comfort His people. Scripture encourages us that every loss has eternal significance, and

God will use every drop of our sorrow for His perfect, grander purposes.

We don't know why God allows specific tragedies to befall us, but we do know that God promises to redeem it all (Romans 8:28). Not only this, but God promises that He is with us. One day, He will return, and He will right every wrong and heal every hurt (Revelation 21:4). Through every hurt, pain, and tragedy in life, we can press into the promise that God is good, and He is coming again. He is with us, and He understands our pain. One day, He will make everything right.

A Letter from Elisabeth Elliot

Elisabeth Elliot, a famous missionary and author, was no stranger to suffering. Her husband was murdered in Ecuador by the tribe he went to serve. After his death, Elisabeth went back with her young child to live among her husband's killers and shared the gospel with them. She later remarried, but her second husband died of cancer. Truly, she knew the pain of sorrow deeply.

In her later years, Elisabeth wrote many books. In one of her books, *Keep a Quiet Heart*, she writes of receiving a letter from a friend who had experienced a miscarriage, tragically losing her daughter, Laura. Elisabeth wrote back, encouraging her friend in the sufferings of Christ and hope of the gospel. We, too, can be encouraged by these words:

> How our hearts were running to you, weeping with you, wishing we could see your faces and tell you our sympathies. Yet it is 'no strange thing' that has happened to you, as Peter said in his epistle (1 Peter 4:12)—it gives you a share in Christ's suffering. To me this is one of the deepest but most comforting of all the mysteries of suffering. Not only does He enter into our grief in the fullest of understanding, suffer with us and for us, but in the very depths of sorrow He allows us, in His mercy, to enter into *His*...

> ...Your dear tiny Laura is in the Shepherd's arms. She will never have to suffer. She knew only the heaven of the womb (the safest place in all the world—apart from the practice of abortion) and now she knows the perfect heaven of God's presence. I'm sure that your prayer for

both your children has been that God would fulfill His purpose in them. It is the highest and best we can ask for our beloved children. He has already answered that prayer for Laura…

…Jesus learned obedience by the things which He suffered, not by the things which He enjoyed. In order to fit you both for His purposes both here and in eternity, He has lent you this sorrow. But He bears the heavier end of the Cross laid upon you! Be sure that Lars and I are praying for you, dear friends.

WAS MY UNBORN BABY A REAL PERSON?

Yes. As Christians, we believe that life exists from the moment of conception (Jeremiah 1:5, Psalm 139:13). Through your miscarriage or stillbirth, you lost a child—a real, beautiful life shaped by your DNA and made in the image of God. When we understand this, we can begin to grieve honestly and mourn before the Lord. You have a right to grieve your loss because your baby was a real person.

Some well-intentioned people may try to comfort you in your grief with phrases like, "Don't worry. You were so early. It probably wasn't even a baby yet." In an attempt to help you feel better, they suggest that the baby wasn't real. Eager for you to feel better, they encourage you to dry your eyes and move on. But ironically, this kind of advice typically doesn't help us feel better. Instead, we feel the loss of life more acutely, but we don't feel permission to mourn with others. Or perhaps you've asked these questions yourself. Sometimes to minimize the enormity of our pain, we look for ways to minimize the significance of the loss. We want to make sense of a seemingly senseless tragedy. To add insult to injury, maybe you weren't able to find out the gender before you miscarried, or you lost your child before you were able to hold him or her. Perhaps your neighbors and co-workers didn't know you were pregnant, and you weren't yet showing. You may feel the pain of loss but question if it's a valid feeling. The memory of your baby feels simultaneously like a vivid loss and a distant dream.

The truth of Psalm 139 reminds us that God forms every life together from the womb. He is the masterful artist, who creates every eyelash, dimple, and freckle. He knit your baby's body together in your womb, forming her personality, body, and spirit. Although you may not have been able to meet your baby this side of heaven, we can rejoice in his or her life, knowing that your baby was carefully and wonderfully made. Even though your baby's life was short, it was not meaningless. His or her life was significantly, beautifully, and wonderfully made.

Isaiah 25:8-9

*When he has swallowed up death
once and for all,
the Lord God will wipe away the tears
from every face
and remove his people's disgrace
from the whole earth,
for the Lord has spoken.*

*On that day it will be said,
"Look, this is our God;
we have waited for him,
and he has saved us.
This is the Lord; we have waited for him.
Let's rejoice and be glad in his salvation.*

WHERE IS THE BABY NOW?

It is natural after the loss of a baby to wonder, *Where is the baby now?* After all, the Scriptures teach us that we are saved through repentance and belief in the gospel. But what about babies who die before they have the capacity to understand the gospel? While there is much debate on this topic among theologians, many point to the verses below to suggest that those who do not have the capacity to hear and understand the gospel will be saved, including babies and infants:

Verses About Salvation, Babies, and God's Sovereignty

It was you who brought me out of the womb, making me secure at my mother's breast. I was given over to you at birth; you have been my God from my mother's womb.
PSALM 22:9-10

In this psalm, David writes about how he was known and called by God from his mother's womb. This verse points us toward God's salvation and care for babies and infants.

He will be filled with the Holy Spirit while still in his mother's womb.
LUKE 1:15B

This verse is about John the Baptist, and it shows that he was filled with the Holy Spirit from the womb. This reality leads us to believe that God's Spirit is able to dwell within the unborn.

Jesus said, "I came into this world for judgment, in order that those who do not see will see and those who do see will

become blind." Some of the Pharisees who were with him heard these things and asked him, "We aren't blind too, are we?" "If you were blind," Jesus told them, "you wouldn't have sin. But now that you say, 'We see,' your sin remains."
JOHN 9:39-41

One principle of Jesus's teaching in John 9 is that God does not unjustly condemn us for what we are unable to do. This gives us hope that God does not condemn infants who are not yet able to understand the gospel.

For his invisible attributes, that is, his eternal power and divine nature, have been clearly seen since the creation of the world, being understood through what he has made. As a result, people are without excuse.
ROMANS 1:20

God has displayed His power and presence through the created world so that all may know Him. Even though we all inherit Adam's sin from birth, infants are unable to see or understand the beauty of creation. This points us to the belief that babies have an excuse against divine judgment because they do not have the capacity to understand what others can by looking at God's creation.

But now that he is dead, why should I fast? Can I bring him back again? I'll go to him, but he will never return to me.
2 SAMUEL 12:23

These words were spoken by King David when his baby died, suggesting the belief that he would see his child again. As those who grieve on this side of eternity, this verse leads us to believe that, like David, we can also hold onto this hope.

Common Questions

While these verses can bring us great hope, there remains much that we cannot fully understand this side of heaven, including pregnancy and infant loss. Still, we can trust God in all things, even regarding salvation, because His character and wisdom are perfect. As Christians, we were saved because of the grace and loving sacrifice of Jesus. God called us from the beginning of time to be His children. He showers us with His love and mercy, not because we've proven our worth to Him but because He is merciful. Truly, no one is saved because he or she deserves it but rather because of God's mercy and grace.

In light of this truth,

you can be confident that God cares about your baby and loves him or her even more than you do.

He is good, gracious, and kind. He does what is perfect. You can trust Him.

Romans 11:33-36

*Oh, the depth of the riches
and the wisdom and the knowledge of God!
How unsearchable his judgments
and untraceable his ways!
For who has known the mind of the Lord?
Or who has been his counselor?
And who has ever given to God,
that he should be repaid?
For from him and through him
and to him are all things.
To him be the glory forever. Amen.*

WILL THIS HAPPEN AGAIN?

As women, it's easy to anticipate tomorrow's troubles. We live in the world of "what-ifs": *What if I miscarry again? What if I'm never able to hold a baby in my arms? What if my husband resents me because of my pregnancy or infant loss?* The "what-ifs" of life consume us. This compounds with the American reality that when young couples get married, they often have a five-year plan, including work, travel, and family planning. There is a deceived sense of control as they make claims such as, "After three years of traveling, working, and enjoying one another, we'll start a family." But sometimes, even with the aid of fertility treatments and doctors, pregnancy does not go as planned. Miscarriages, stillbirths, sickness, and death remind us that we are not in control.

Although we do not know what tomorrow holds, we know the One who does.

God is good, and He plans our future. He orders and protects the world. He loves us and cares for our every need. While we do not always understand why God allows certain trials in our lives, we remember that He is in control, and He loves us. He holds every tomorrow in His hands, and He is a good Father who gives good gifts. We can trust in His goodness, knowing that He will make all things right.

As Christians, we have seen the goodness of the Lord firsthand. God has adopted us as His children and rescued us from sin and darkness. He has blessed us with His Spirit to guide us, and He has given us air to breathe and His creation to enjoy. He has placed us in families and provided His body, the Church, to care for us. He has taken care of every eternal need; surely we can trust Him with our future, knowing that He will never leave or forsake us (Hebrews 13:5).

> *When we anxiously worry about tomorrow, we use today's energy on tomorrow's problems.*

As Eric Bancroft, pastor of Grace Church in Miami, once said in a sermon, we live as future atheists, forgetting that God is real and that He will be there tomorrow to help us. As Christians, we can live with real and lasting hope, not because we are promised a specific blessing in the future, but because we have assurance in God's presence and character. We are not in control, but God is; He can be trusted. He is the King of the universe, the Maker of heaven and earth, your loving Father, and He will help you.

Matthew 6:25-34

"Therefore I tell you: Don't worry about your life, what you will eat or what you will drink; or about your body, what you will wear. Isn't life more than food and the body more than clothing? Consider the birds of the sky: They don't sow or reap or gather into barns, yet your heavenly Father feeds them. Aren't you worth more than they? Can any of you add one moment to his life span by worrying? And why do you worry about clothes? Observe how the wildflowers of the field grow: They don't labor or spin thread. Yet I tell you that not even Solomon in all his splendor was adorned like one of these. If that's how God clothes the grass of the field, which is here today and thrown into the furnace tomorrow, won't he do much more for you—you of little faith? So don't worry, saying, 'What will we eat?' or 'What will we drink?' or 'What will we wear?' For the Gentiles eagerly seek all these things, and your heavenly Father knows that you need them. But seek first the kingdom of God and his righteousness, and all these things will be provided for you. Therefore don't worry about tomorrow, because tomorrow will worry about itself. Each day has enough trouble of its own."

List Your Fears

Make a list of your fears of the future:

_____
_____
_____
_____
_____
_____
_____
_____
_____
_____
_____
_____
_____

After you have finished, pray and surrender these fears to the Lord. Ask for faith to trust Him, and remember that He will be with you to help you always, even if one of your worst fears comes true. Share your list with a trusted friend or family member, and search the Scriptures to see what God, through His Word, has to say about your fears.

WILL THE PAIN EVER END?

Yes. One day, God will mend our broken hearts and bind up our wounds. Every pain and sorrow will be healed. Today, you may be sick with grief and consumed with longing, the dreams of what could have been filling your mind. You wonder: *What would I have looked like fully pregnant? What was the baby like? What would he or she have looked like or enjoyed? Would he love trucks, balls, or dinosaurs? Would she love ballet, piano, or soccer?*

But it will not always be this way.

In time, God will bring comfort, healing, peace, and joy to the broken crevices of your heart.

In time, as you grieve openly and honestly before the Lord, you will find that the sharp sting of death will fade. You won't need to fake a smile at your niece's birthday party, and you won't have to fight to get out of bed each Mother's Day. The pain of grief will change, and when this healing begins to happen, it does not mean that you've forgotten your baby or that you don't still miss her. It also doesn't mean that you'll be immune to grief pangs, moments when memories of loss seem as fresh as if they just occurred. Rather, in time, God will begin to heal your heart and bring hope for tomorrow. You will find that you've gone days without tears, that you've started to make plans again for the future. You will be able to envision happier days and enjoy the gifts the Lord has given you today. The light of morning will come again.

When we feel the pain of death, we remember that it wasn't supposed to be this way. When God made the world, He designed it free from death and decay.

And one day, He will come to restore and redeem the world. One day, we will be reunited with our Maker and Father. When Jesus comes back, He will wipe every tear and heal every hurt. He will restore every brokenness, and He will make everything right.

As we await this future hope, we remember that God is with us, even in the most tragic moments of life.

Through sorrow, pain, and grief, we discover that Christ is our greatest, unfading treasure

—greater than any gift, person, or relationship.

Our Savior is enough for us, and He will never leave us or forsake us. He is worthy of our devotion and affection, even through tear-stained cheeks and aching prayers. He promises to heal our hearts with His true and lasting peace.

How Firm a Foundation

How firm a foundation, ye saints of the Lord,
is laid for your faith in His excellent Word!
What more can He say than to you He hath said,
who unto the Savior for refuge have fled?

"In ev'ry condition, in sickness, in health,
in poverty's vale, or abounding in wealth,
at home and abroad, on the land, on the sea,
as days may demand, shall thy strength ever be."

"Fear not, I am with thee, O be not dismayed,
for I am thy God and will still give thee aid.
I'll strengthen thee, help thee, and cause thee to stand,
upheld by My righteous, omnipotent hand."

"When through the deep waters I call thee to go,
the rivers of sorrow shall not overflow;
for I will be with thee, thy troubles to bless,
and sanctify to thee thy deepest distress."

"When through fiery trials thy pathway shall lie,
My grace, all-sufficient, shall be thy supply.
The flame shall not hurt thee; I only design
thy dross to consume, and thy gold to refine."

"The soul that on Jesus hath leaned for repose
I will not, I will not desert to his foes;
that soul, though all hell should endeavor to shake,
I'll never, no never, no never forsake!"

In time, God will begin to heal your heart and bring hope for tomorrow.

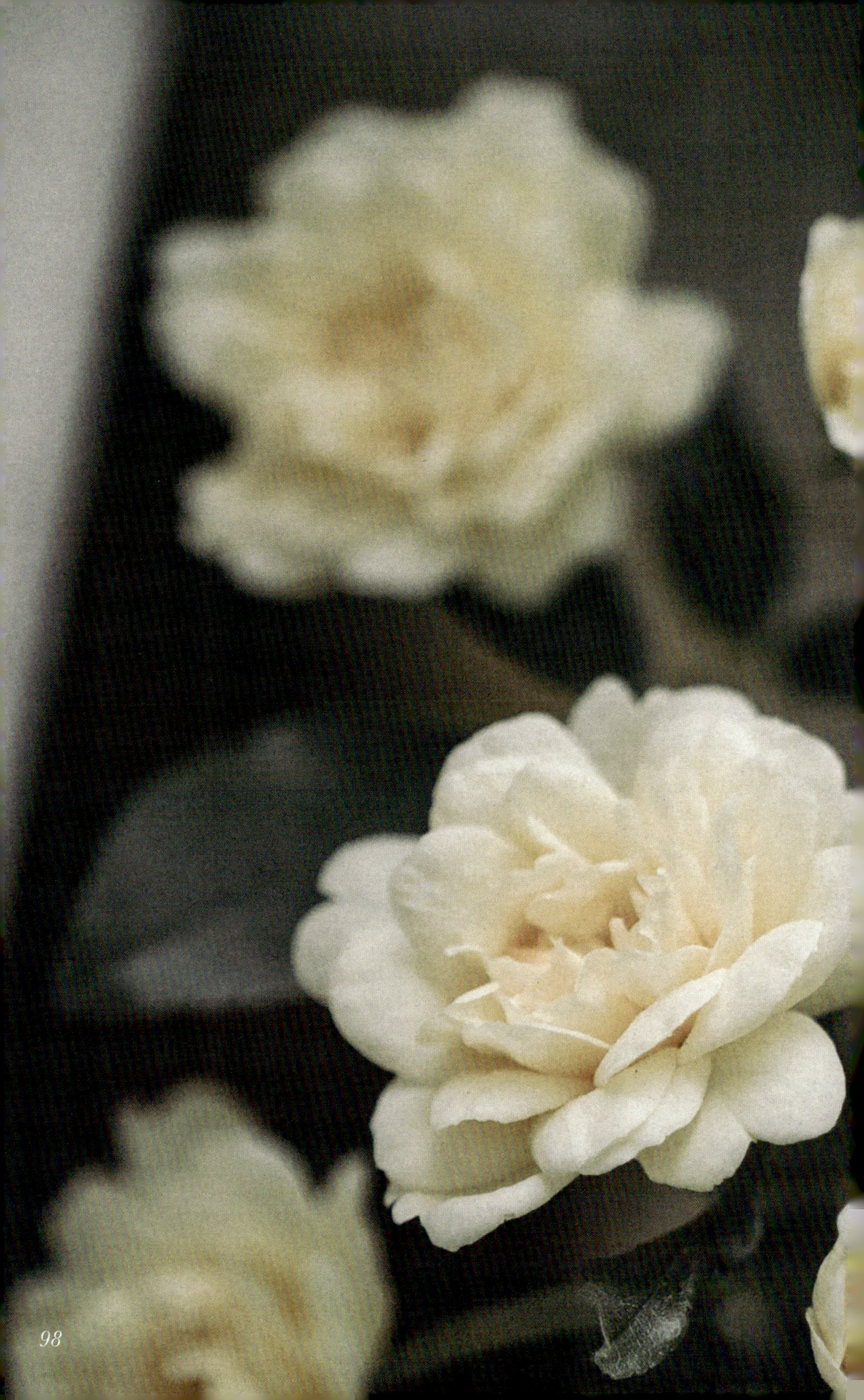

Through sorrow, pain, and grief, we discover that Christ is our greatest, unfading treasure.

05.
Family Planning After Pregnancy or Infant Loss

PREGNANCY AFTER MISCARRIAGE, STILLBIRTH, OR INFANT LOSS

ADOPTION AFTER MISCARRIAGE, STILLBIRTH, OR INFANT LOSS

SECONDARY INFERTILITY

PREGNANCY AFTER MISCARRIAGE, STILLBIRTH, OR INFANT LOSS

You are pregnant again! After months of trying to conceive, you hold your breath in disbelief as two pink lines slowly form on a tiny, white stick. Your body instantly recognizes the familiarity of this season, and you feel life beginning to grow inside you. But this time, you feel more nervous, cautious, and apprehensive. Maybe you don't want to tell your family that you're pregnant until after the first trimester, or maybe you choose to tell your family immediately so that they can be praying for the baby. You want to see the doctor as soon as possible and get more tests to confirm the increasing hCG levels within you. You want to know that death won't happen again. After all, you know the pain of leaving the hospital empty-handed and the anguish of milk coming in with no baby to feed. You feel anxious yet hopeful about the baby growing within you.

Every life is a gift, but after losing a baby due to pregnancy or infant loss, it is normal to experience lingering fear in subsequent pregnancies. With a new baby, our minds run incessantly, playing out every possible scenario and trying to brace ourselves for the worst. This is natural, especially if your pregnancy or infant loss affected you severely.

A positive pregnancy test does not erase grief. Instead, for those who have experienced loss, it often produces a hesitant hope. Yet, even when we do not know what tomorrow holds, we can trust that God is in control over all things. We do not need to fear because we know the One who holds every tomorrow in His hands. He has good plans for us, and He will accomplish His perfect, loving purposes. Find comfort in God's words to His people, found in Isaiah 41:10:

> Do not fear, for I am with you;
> do not be afraid, for I am your God.
> I will strengthen you; I will help you;
> I will hold on to you with my
> righteous right hand.

God tells His people not to fear, not because He promises them a problem-free life but because He is with them. In the same way, God promises to care for and strengthen you in every season. Even if the worst-case scenario should come to pass, God is still in control, and He will help you. He is still good. He holds you with His strong, righteous right hand, and He will help you. We can thank God for the blessings that He gives — even when we do not know the future — because He is with us.

Amazingly, God has made you a mother again through pregnancy. You can joyfully praise God for the gift of this baby. At the same time, it is okay to feel conflicting emotions. Make a mindful effort to process these emotions before the Lord in prayer, and verbally share your thoughts with your spouse, friends, and/or a biblical counselor. Meditate on Scriptures such as Psalm 46, remembering that God is our refuge and strength, a very present help in trouble. Recite the words of Psalm 16, which remind us that the Lord is our portion and our cup; we have no good thing apart from Him. Meditate on what is true, even as you wait upon the Lord.

You can trust God with your future because He is with you. You can trust God with your baby because He loves you. God is your refuge, comfort, and strength. He will never abandon you, and He has good plans for you. He is our hope for today and tomorrow, our only hope in life and death.

Philippians 4:6–7

Don't worry about anything, but in everything, through prayer and petition with thanksgiving, present your requests to God. And the peace of God, which surpasses all understanding, will guard your hearts and minds in Christ Jesus.

We do not need to fear because we know the One who holds every tomorrow in His hands.

ADOPTION AFTER MISCARRIAGE, STILLBIRTH, OR INFANT LOSS

Adoption is a beautiful reflection of the love of God. As Christians, we were adopted into the family of our heavenly Father. Though we were orphans, without hope or a future, God had mercy on us and made us heirs of the King. He invited us into His family and chose us to be His children. He adopted us as sons and daughters. In light of this redemption truth, many men and women choose to imitate the love of the Father by growing their families through the adoption of children. This can be an incredible way to become parents to a beautiful child.

For those who have experienced pregnancy or infant loss, it is important to recognize that adoption does not erase the pain of death or infertility. Instead, the process of adoption can often bring out lingering feelings of inadequacy, fear, or loss. In an adoption, prospective adoptive families often must complete interviews with caseworkers. They must prove that they would be good parents and, at times, need to "sell themselves" to prospective birth parents. This can be difficult for couples who have experienced pregnancy or infant loss. Having gone through so many heartaches already, they simply want to become parents. Not only this, but some prospective adoptive families begin the process of adoption because of the myth that if they fill out the adoption application, they will soon get pregnant. When this fails to come true, they are devastated.

If you choose to pursue adoption, recognize that the adoptive process will not remove your feelings of grief. It is important to work through lingering feelings of doubt, insecurity, or incompleteness and not expect that an adoption will heal your grieving heart. As you continue through the adoption process, have honest conversations with families who have adopted. Ask good questions, and create a foundation of realistic expectations for the adoption process. Interview adoption agencies, and inquire about their training and counseling services. Many adoption agencies offer support and training for women who have experienced loss as well.

Throughout it all, take heart.

God desires to bring healing, hope, and purpose out of your suffering.

He makes everything beautiful in His time (Ecclesiastes 3:11), and He has a great plan for you. If the Lord leads you to become a parent through adoption, your child will be a beautiful gift to you. Adoption is a wonderful way to become parents and joyfully engage in the mission of God. Just as God adopted us as His children, we too can welcome children into our homes and call them sons and daughters.

Ephesians 1:3–6

Blessed is the God and Father of our Lord Jesus Christ, who has blessed us with every spiritual blessing in the heavens in Christ. For he chose us in him, before the foundation of the world, to be holy and blameless in love before him. He predestined us to be adopted as sons through Jesus Christ for himself, according to the good pleasure of his will, to the praise of his glorious grace that he lavished on us in the Beloved One.

Adoption is a beautiful reflection of the love of God.

SECONDARY INFERTILITY

Maybe you already have several children at home. You never experienced a single problem with your pregnancies—until now. Now, you long to get pregnant again, but you wait month after month without getting pregnant. Your family and friends tell you to be thankful for the kids you have, to look on the bright side, yet you long for more. Your family feels incomplete.

Secondary infertility is defined as having trouble conceiving after giving birth to another child. According to the United States Department of Health and Human Services, approximately six million women have trouble becoming pregnant or staying pregnant, and one-third of these experience secondary infertility. Secondary infertility can be a surprising form of grief, especially if you have gotten pregnant easily in the past. The surprise mixed with the grief and disappointment can be shocking and overwhelming.

Having children in the home does not remove the pain of infertility. The human heart is complex, and we can simultaneously be thankful for the blessings that God has given us while also grieving desires unfulfilled. In the Bible, Rachel experienced this kind of complex longing firsthand. After a long season of infertility, she gave birth to a son and named him Joseph. Yet, even after God blessed her with one son, she still longed for another. This is reflected in Joseph's name, which means "He will add." After giving birth, Rachel prayed, "May the Lord add another son to me" (Genesis 30:24). Similarly, it is natural to rejoice in the children God has given you while longing for another child at the same time.

Scripture calls children a blessing, and a desire for another child can be a beautiful longing. Yet, while we can pray for a child through birth or adoption, we cannot predict or control the plans of the Lord. God is the giver of life, the Creator of every man, woman, and child. Our unfulfilled longings for another child remind us of this truth—that we are not in control. But thankfully, we know the One who is, and He is good. Even when God says "no" or "not now" to our desires, we know that He is doing something greater than we could imagine. God promises to be with us in our troubles and to use them for our good. He is a good Father who grows our faith and strengthens our endurance. He amplifies our love for others and refines us into His image. Not only this, but He reminds us that He is greater than every gift. He is greater than the gift of another snuggly toddler hug, and He is greater than a fulfilling Mother's Day with an extra plate at the table. He is the longing of our hearts, the only One who can truly satisfy.

Even in a season of waiting, Scripture calls us to consider these temporary trials as joy because God is working in them. We can grieve desires unfulfilled and pour out our hearts before the Lord while resting in the truth that this suffering is not meaningless. You are not lesser of a woman because you are unable to get pregnant. Your life is not waiting to begin. God is fully pleased with you in Christ. He has great plans for you.

You have a loving Father who guides your every step, and He will sustain you in this season of waiting.

1 Peter 1:3-7

Blessed be the God and Father of our Lord Jesus Christ. Because of his great mercy he has given us new birth into a living hope through the resurrection of Jesus Christ from the dead and into an inheritance that is imperishable, undefiled, and unfading, kept in heaven for you. You are being guarded by God's power through faith for a salvation that is ready to be revealed in the last time. You rejoice in this, even though now for a short time, if necessary, you suffer grief in various trials so that the proven character of your faith—more valuable than gold which, though perishable, is refined by fire—may result in praise, glory, and honor at the revelation of Jesus Christ.

God is the giver of life, the Creator of every man, woman, and child.

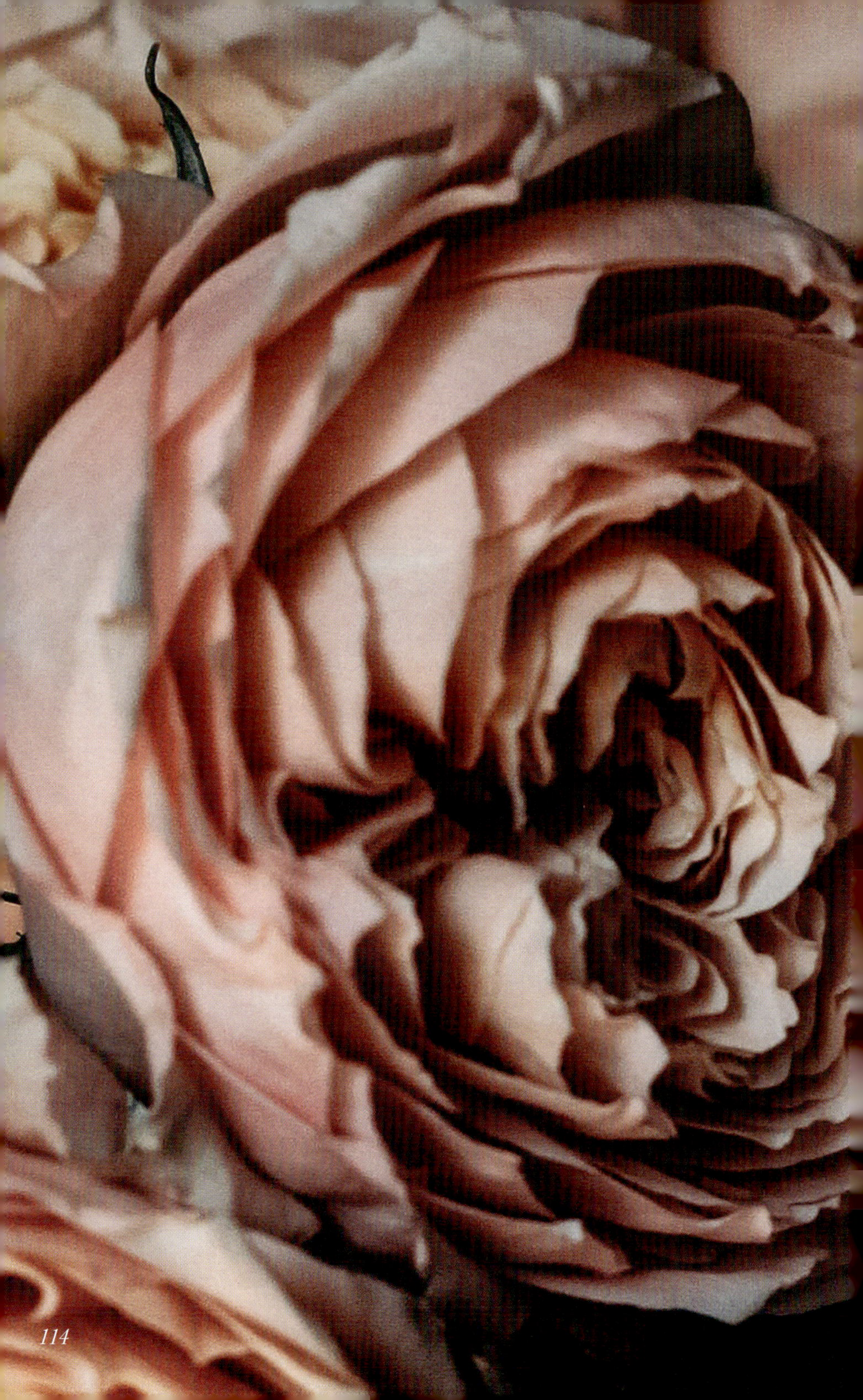

We are not in control. But thankfully, we know the One who is, and He is good.

ern # 06.

Processing Pregnancy or Infant Loss With Others

SHOW GRACE

GUARD AGAINST BITTERNESS

FIND TRUSTED FRIENDS

PROCESSING PREGNANCY OR
INFANT LOSS WITH YOUR CHILDREN

PROCESSING PREGNANCY OR
INFANT LOSS WITH YOUR SPOUSE

SHOW GRACE

Many people often don't know how to respond to loss. They want to say the right thing and comfort you in your pain, but they don't know how. Sometimes, they avoid mentioning the baby because they don't want to make you sad. At other times, they say insensitive comments in an attempt to cheer you up. Perhaps they don't understand the extent of your pain or have never experienced the loss of a loved one. They unknowingly aggravate your pain and intensify your sense of loss through their words, actions, or behaviors.

As much as possible, show grace to those around you. Ask God to help you communicate honestly but with compassion and grace. If someone asks an insensitive or invasive question, you can always respond that you don't feel comfortable answering their question. Or, if someone makes an insensitive comment, you can choose to ignore it or speak the truth in love.

For example, a friend in your life could say something insensitive like, "At least you know you are able to get pregnant," or "Well, maybe the baby had a deformity, and this was God sparing you from hardship." Depending on the circumstance and person, you may choose to simply overlook the offense, forgiving their ignorance or hurtful words. Or, you may decide to lovingly respond to their consolations, saying something such as, "Yes, that is true, but we are still grieving the baby that we lost." Or, "Yes, that may be true, but it's not helpful for me to think about that in this season when I'm currently grieving what we've lost. Can you be praying that I would trust that God is good even through loss?" As much as possible, do not respond to the insensitivity of others with sinful anger. Be kind and compassionate, even as your family and friends learn how to love you as you grieve.

As believers, God has forgiven us of every sin we've ever committed. He has shown us great mercy and canceled our debt through the blood of His Son. In light of this, let us show grace to our friends and family members as they learn how to communicate about loss.

Ephesians 4:32

And be kind and compassionate to one another, forgiving one another, just as God also forgave you in Christ.

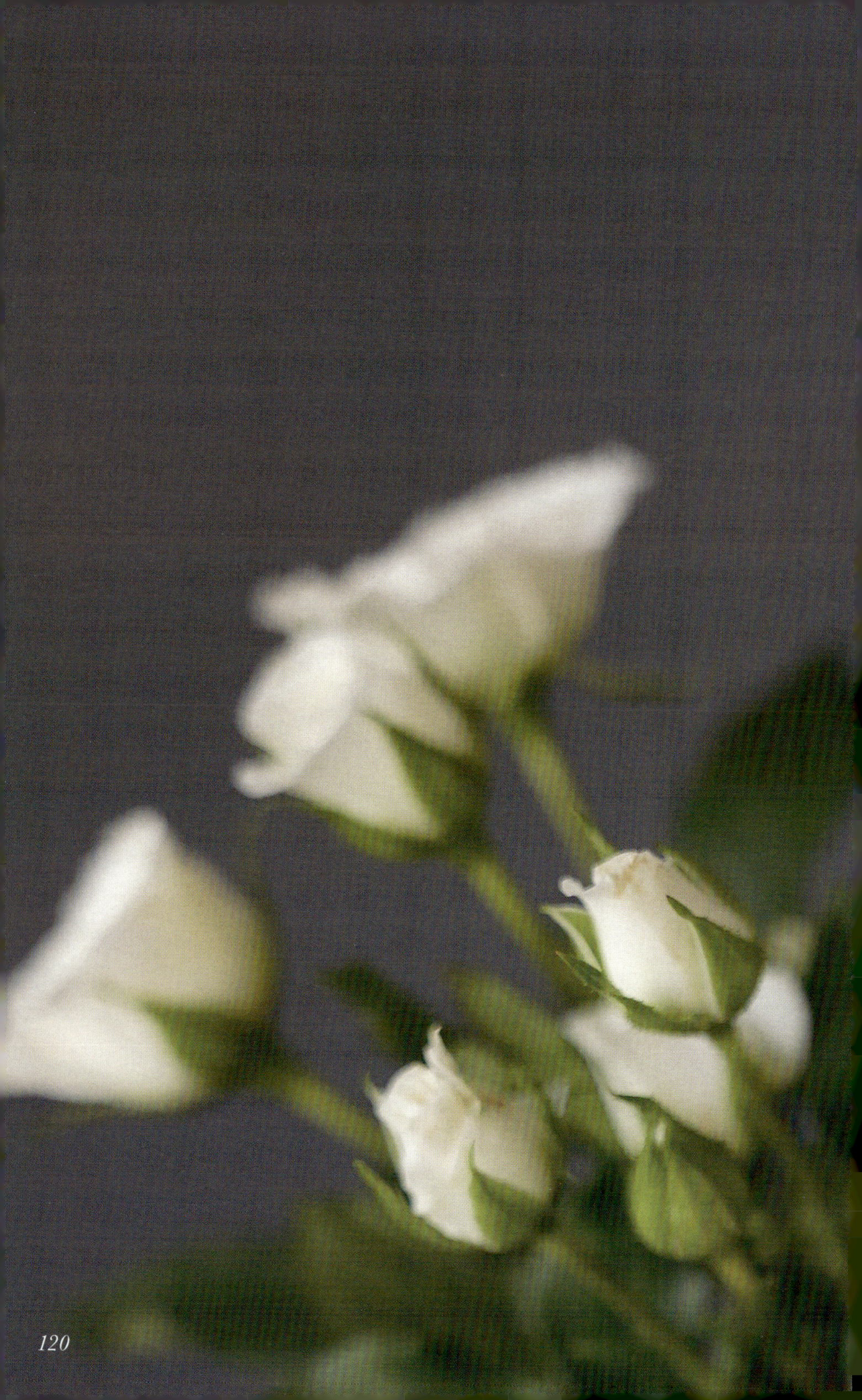

Be kind and compassionate, even as your family and friends learn how to love you as you grieve.

GUARD AGAINST BITTERNESS

After a pregnancy or infant loss, God can feel distant, cruel, and unloving. Every weekend, it seems like you attend a new baby shower, while your womb remains empty. Many of your friends have announced their pregnancies online, yet you ache with longing for a baby. When we are disappointed, it is easy to let the root of bitterness creep into our hearts. What begins as a longing to be pregnant can, over time, settle into resentment, bitterness, distance in relationships, and despair.

Ask God to help you guard your heart. Even when seemingly all of your friends become pregnant and it feels as if your days are heavy with tears, remember: God has not forgotten you. Your life is not empty, and He has great purposes for you. Every one of your days was designed for His glorious purposes, and He will supply all that you need in Christ. He is enough for us.

Expect that many "firsts" will be difficult: the first Christmas, the first New Year's, the first birthday, or the first pregnancy announcement of a friend after the loss. On these days, you may find it is especially difficult to seek contentment when many of your friends have the kind of life you desire. It may be helpful to disconnect from social media for a season or find a biblical counselor with whom you can process these emotions. Guard your heart and your mind by dwelling on what is true, meditating on Scripture, listening to worship music, and fighting for joy.

You are not alone. While there are stories of victory in pregnancy, such as Sarah and Hannah in the Bible, there are many faithful women who have had their desires delayed. When God says "no," or delays in answering our prayers with a "yes," we have the opportunity to discover that Christ is enough for us. He will sustain us and show our fragile hearts that He is greater than every good gift, even your desire to be a mother. Press into Him. He alone can satisfy, and at His right hand are pleasures forevermore (Psalm 16:11). His character is trustworthy, and His promises are good.

Hebrews 12:14-15

Pursue peace with everyone, and holiness—without it no one will see the Lord. Make sure that no one falls short of the grace of God and that no root of bitterness springs up, causing trouble and defiling many.

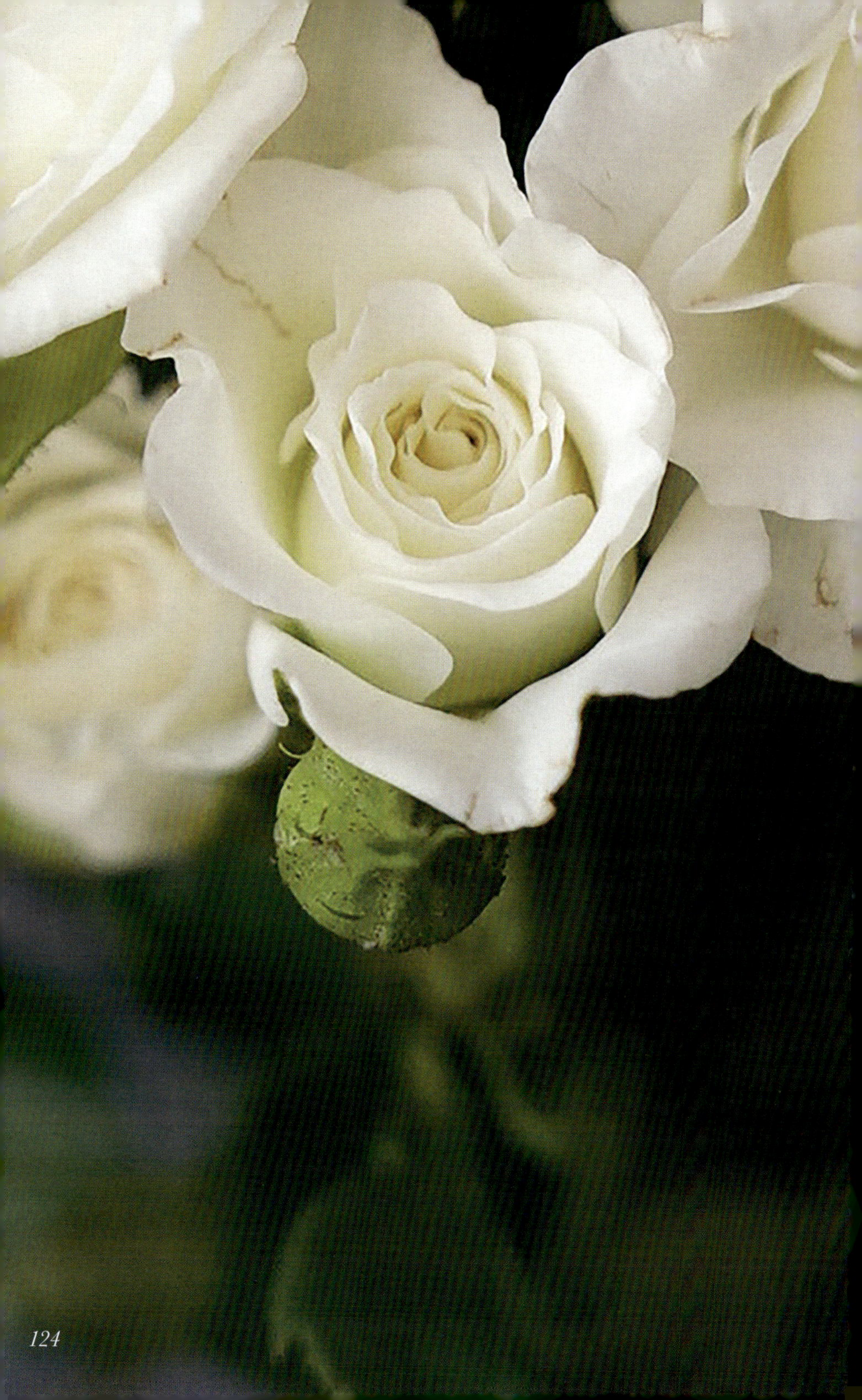

Remember: God has not forgotten you. Your life is not empty, and He has great purposes for you.

FIND TRUSTED FRIENDS

As you navigate the hurtful comments of some, find trusted friends who can encourage you—friends who will not judge you in your grief but with whom you can express honest laments, doubts, pain, and concerns. Friends who will pray for you, cry with you, and encourage you. A true friend will not only empathize with your pain—she will also pray for you and remind you of the truth. She will hold you up when you fall (Ecclesiastes 4:10) and pray for you when you are discouraged (Job 42:10). She will not gossip about you (Proverbs 17:9) but will offer loving advice based on the truths of God's Word (Proverbs 27:9). She will encourage you to trust the Lord when your faith feels weak.

It's okay to ask for help. As you process your grief, rely on your friends and family members, and reach out for help. Ask for help in your daily life, whether taking care of your older children or attending doctor's appointments. Ask friends to periodically check in with you to ask how you are doing. Ask for accountability to be in the Word, pray, and attend church. But not only this, as you are seeking to find these trusted friends, aim to become this friend for others. As the sting of grief softens, seek to become a sister who joyfully carries the burdens of others out of love for them and love for Christ (Galatians 6:2).

God has not designed us to live our lives on our own.

Find trusted brothers or sisters in Christ who can care for you in your grief and who you can love and support as well.

Verses About Friendship

> For if either falls, his companion can
> lift him up; but pity the one who falls
> without another to lift him up.
>
> **ECCLESIASTES 4:10**

> "This is my command: Love one another as
> I have loved you. No one has greater love than
> this: to lay down his life for his friends."
>
> **JOHN 15:12–13**

> One with many friends may be
> harmed, but there is a friend who
> stays closer than a brother.
>
> **PROVERBS 18:24**

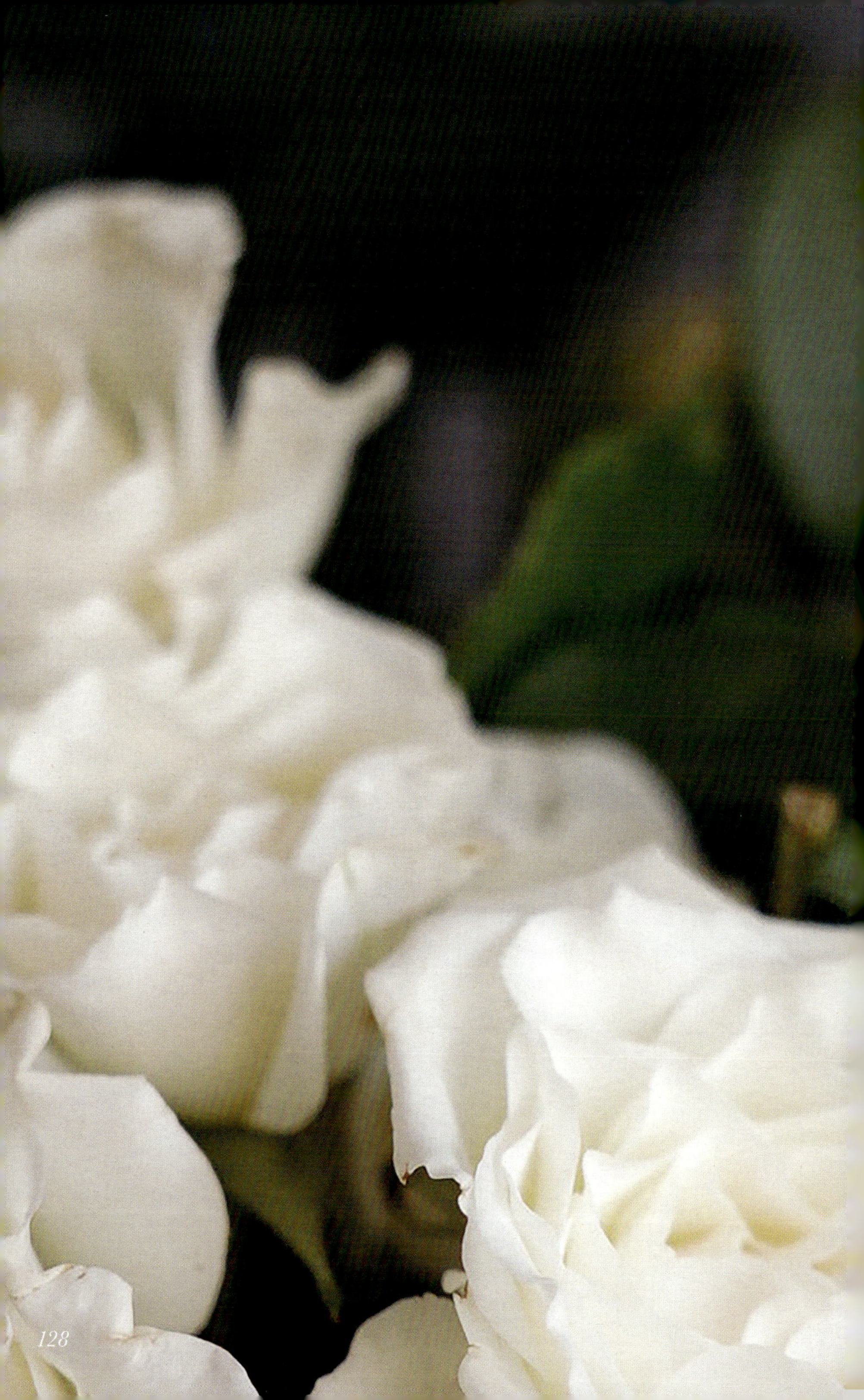

As the sting of grief softens, seek to become a sister who joyfully carries the burdens of others.

PROCESSING PREGNANCY OR INFANT LOSS WITH YOUR CHILDREN

If you have children in the home, your pregnancy or infant loss affects not only you and your husband. It also affects your older children who experienced the loss of a sibling. As a parent, you love your children and want to help them process through the loss of their baby brother or sister. But you may feel ill-equipped or insecure about how to help them. Although it can be difficult to comfort someone else while you are grieving, try to give your children the opportunity to express how they are feeling.

This season is an opportunity for you to grow closer as a family.

Younger children often process grief through play. They may color pictures of their mommy crying or draw bubbles of their baby brother in heaven. They may play with their dolls, imagining doctor's appointments or quiet, "boring" days. Consider entering into their play worlds to help them process. Pick up a mommy doll, enter into their imaginary world, and ask the other baby doll how she is doing. Or color a happy face, sad face, angry face, and confused face, and ask your child which one he or she is feeling. If your children are very young, they may not understand the concept of death or a baby growing in mommy's belly. That's okay. You don't need to force them to recognize the loss before they are developmentally ready.

Older children may have many questions about the baby. They may grapple with big questions about God's goodness or sovereignty. Give them an opportunity to ask hard questions, and don't ignore your children's concerns. As much as possible, answer your children's questions honestly and simply. If you don't know the answer to a difficult question, it's okay to say, "I don't know."

As you process the loss as a family, you may discover that your children respond differently to the loss. Some children may think that the death is their fault. They may feel guilty because they were not more excited about the baby. They may wonder if God is punishing them for something. Be sensitive to how your child is processing the pregnancy or infant loss, and provide a safe space to process together. Other kids may try to be good or strong in response to the loss, inwardly carrying feelings of sadness and guilt but trying to help their mom feel better. Still other children may respond through anger. They may rebel, missing the attention and affection of their parents, which has been muted by grief. In any scenario, try to be a safe person for your child to talk to. Allow your child to process the loss at his or her own pace. Help them learn to verbalize and name their emotions so that they can grow in their emotional development and find the hope of the Scriptures for that emotion.

Although it is easy to let the pain of a pregnancy or infant loss consume your world, try to plan times together as a family, and check in periodically with your children to see how they are doing. Create opportunities to talk, and plan outings or activities together. Brainstorm traditions you can do together to remember the baby.

As a parent, you are your children's primary discipler. Even through your grief, you can communicate to your children that it's okay to be sad and that they can pray to God even when they're mad, disappointed, or scared. God does not expect you to be a perfect parent in your grief. Rather,

amid this loss, you have the opportunity, even through pain, to point your children to God.

You can teach your children how to pray honest prayers. You can model good communication and what it looks like to rely on biblical community. Throughout your children's lives, they will face disappointments. You have the unique opportunity to lead your children to the throne of God and teach them how to trust God during times of trouble.

HELPING YOUR CHILDREN
Process the Loss of a Sibling

Consider the following practical steps to help your children grieve the loss of a sibling:

FOR YOUNGER CHILDREN:

- If age-appropriate, explain in simple words to your child that you had a baby in your belly who died, and that makes you sad. Some children may be too young to understand the loss. That's okay. You do not need to make them understand before they are ready.

- Some children may feel guilty or wonder if they are not enough since their mom is so sad. Tell your child that you love him or her and that you are happy he or she is your son or daughter.

- Enter into your child's world through coloring or play. Leave room for your child to ask questions, but don't expect your child to fully understand the gravity of the loss.

- Observe any changes in your child, and seek advice from older mothers who have experienced grief.

- Be patient through tantrums and/or unusual patterns of behavior. As much as possible, try to maintain your previous normal rhythms and routines. When this is impossible, communicate with your child that the next few weeks will look a little different. You may say something like, "Mommy is sad about the baby, so the next few weeks may look a little different. We may have family visiting, and you may get some extra screen time. I want you to know that even if Mommy spends some time crying or even if I spend some extra time by myself, I love you so much. I am so proud of you and am so glad that you are my son."

- Show your child an emotions chart of smiley faces showing different emotions. Ask your child to point to the face that describes how he or she feels. Name that emotion (sad, mad, confused, happy), and ask why your child feels that way.

- Younger children may ask the same questions over and over. As much as possible, continue to love them and help them process through their loss.

FOR OLDER CHILDREN:

- Although it is difficult, don't completely hide your pain from your older children.

- Ask your child how he or she is processing the loss, and share about your pain. If possible, share about the hope that you have in Christ. Share that though you don't understand why this has happened, you are trying to preach the gospel to yourself by reminding yourself that God is still good. Use this as an opportunity to point to the hope of Christ—that God is with you and is coming again to make all things right.

- Take care of your body, and model healthy communication with your spouse and friends. Take the time you need to grieve. Find trusted friends and/or a biblical counselor to help you process your loss. Take care of your health so that you can love your family well.

- Plan opportunities to talk as a family with intentional questions. If appropriate, make plans for lighthearted activities outside of the home as well so that your child does not feel like he or she needs to match your level of sadness in order to grieve well.

- Consider asking questions such as: What do you think the baby would have been like? Were there any activities you were wanting to do with your sibling? When are you most disappointed about not having a baby brother or baby sister?

- Plan ways to remember the baby as a family. This may include a tradition, buying a stocking for Christmas for the baby, or mentioning the baby by name.

- Have a ceremony, or plan a time to say goodbye to the baby. If applicable, ask your child if they would like to say a prayer or read a poem to honor the baby.

- Pray for your children and with your children. Pray that God would guide your words and help you share the loss with hope. Pray that God would use this tragedy to draw them closer to the gospel and saving faith in Christ.

In grief, we have the opportunity to grow closer together or to push against one another in our pain.

PROCESSING PREGNANCY OR INFANT LOSS WITH YOUR SPOUSE

A miscarriage, stillbirth, or infant loss can be difficult on your marriage. Maybe you saw the look on your husband's face when he heard the news of the loss. He looked so devastated, and ever since, he has withdrawn into his own world. Grief has formed an invisible wall between you and your husband. Or maybe, your husband seemed dispassionate and unconnected from the baby. It feels like he doesn't care that his baby died. He's continued with life and work as if nothing happened. You feel disconnected, isolated, and alone in your marriage.

Every person responds to the loss of a baby differently. Not only this, but men and women who experience the loss of a child often respond in dramatically different ways. Some men feel the pain of pregnancy or infant loss to the same extent—or even to greater degrees—than their wives. Others feel disconnected from a child they were never able to hold, see, or touch. Some men process their grief inwardly or put up a wall in an emotional attempt to be strong for their wives. Others may feel incompetent or ashamed because they were unable to protect their wives from pain. Meanwhile, women are more likely to feel the loss deeply, accept blame for the loss, and take on the stress of a pregnancy or infant loss.

In grief, we have the opportunity to grow closer together or to push against one another in our pain. As you process the loss within your marriage, consider the sample ideas on the following pages to grow closer to your spouse in the midst of grief.

- Ask your spouse how you can be loving and supporting him in his season of grief.

- Tell your spouse how he can help you in moments of intense grief. Be specific with examples such as, "When I am crying, I usually don't want to talk or problem-solve. I just want a hug," or "When you say you'll love me even if we can never have a baby, it makes me feel like you've given up hope." After you let him know how you are feeling, make sure you allow space for him to explain his feelings as well.

- Take time to grieve separately and together. Give your spouse the opportunity to process on his own, and plan times to talk about how each of you is doing.

- Talk together about how you would like to celebrate the life of your baby. Make plans for birthdays, anniversaries, or other important dates.

- There is often not a lot of support for men after pregnancy or infant loss. Their friends often do not know what to say, and many men feel especially lonely or ashamed. Provide a safe space for your husband to share how he is responding to the loss of his child.

- Remind your spouse when an important day is coming up, and talk through your plans for the day ahead of time.

- Some men emotionally disconnect or go into problem-solving mode after their wives experience pregnancy or infant loss. Ask your spouse to share how he has been processing the loss.

- Highlight sections of this booklet that you identify with, and ask your spouse to read them so that he can better understand how you are processing this loss. Ask him to highlight any sections that resonate with him so that you can better understand what he is feeling.

- Tell your spouse if you want to talk about the baby but feel discouraged from doing so because it seems to make others uncomfortable.

- Consider: Are you moving toward your spouse or away from him? Choose the right time to have a loving conversation about your current levels of emotional, spiritual, and physical intimacy.

- Share your loss with your local pastor as a couple.

- Seek a trusted biblical counselor together.

- Share the specific dreams and desires you had for your baby. Express how great your spouse would have been as a father.

- Pray for your spouse, regardless of how he is processing the loss externally. Pray that your marriage would remain strong, pray that your faith would grow, and pray that the grief would push you together rather than pull you apart.

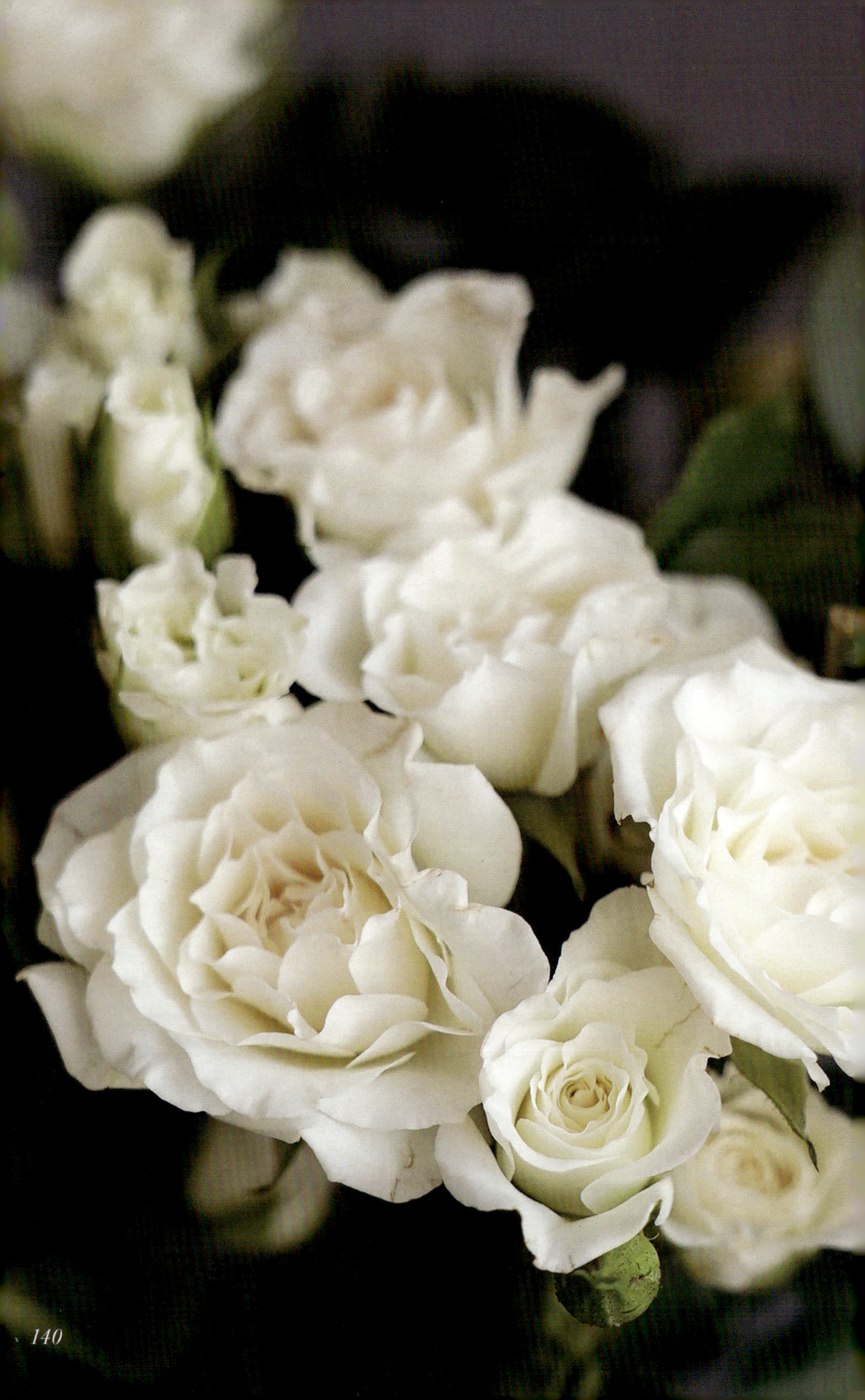

Pray that the grief would push you together rather than pull you apart.

07.

How to Help Those Who Have Experienced Loss

BE A FRIEND

PRAY

OFFER TANGIBLE SUPPORT

MENTION THE BABY'S NAME

WHAT NOT TO SAY

WHAT TO SAY

How to Help Those Who Have Experienced Loss

BE A FRIEND

If your friend or loved one has experienced pregnancy or infant loss, ask God to help you be a good friend to her. Learn to love her in her season of grief by asking good questions and being a good listener. Seek to be patient and kind, expressing your care to her in both word and deed.

One way to show love for our friends is through the ministry of presence. God didn't just love us from afar, but He came close through the incarnation. He sent His Son, Jesus, to leave the splendors of heaven and come to earth, to live with us, get dirty with us, eat with us, and cry with us. In the same way, we can love our friends and family members by entering into their moments of grief and being with them in person.

Practically speaking, one way to love your friend is to show up for her when she needs you, and keep showing up. Show up to the hospital, and show up if there is a funeral. Show up for the moments she needs prayer, and show up for the moments she is sad. Be a source of patient, consistent, and loving care for your friend.

Often after a loss, a hurting friend can be disconnected or even, at times, angry. She may say hurtful words or doubt God's presence in her life. As much as possible, be patient with her, and gently love her through her grief. Do not expect her to "bounce back" from the loss quickly, and do not become discouraged when she does not feel better with your comforting words. Instead, be a reliable friend who lets her share honestly and doesn't condemn her for her grief. Pray for your friend, and encourage her.

PRAY

If we desire to help our grieving friends, we must be praying for them. Although we cannot bring true peace and healing to our friends' souls, God can. He is with them at all times, sustaining and caring for them. He is our refuge, strength, and hope. He is our comfort, Savior, and closest friend. Praying for those we love is one important way to help them in their grief. Pray not only that their suffering would end, but also ask God to give them the grace they need to trust Him in the midst of their trials. Pray that He would sustain them in their daily activities and bring emotional, spiritual, and physical healing.

When our friends are grieving, we can pray for:

- Faith to trust God when life hurts
- The courage to honestly lament before the Lord
- Comfort and strength
- Healing and relief from pain
- Protection
- Endurance
- Community to hold her up when her faith is weak
- Greater dependence on the Lord in prayer
- A trust in God that covers her fears

- Mental clarity in daily activities
- Strength to love her husband and/or other children well
- Wisdom in making decisions, from doctor's appointments to funeral arrangements
- Opportunities to serve others
- Gospel witness to unbelieving neighbors, friends, and family members
- That God's Word would be her rock and comfort
- The ability to dwell on what is true
- Physical health
- Emotional health
- Spiritual health
- Wisdom for you to know how to love and serve her
- _____

(Write in specific prayer requests for your friend)

- _____
- _____
- _____
- _____
- _____
- _____

Write a Prayer for Your Friend

Use the section below to write a prayer
for your grieving friend:

_____
_____
_____
_____
_____
_____
_____
_____
_____
_____
_____
_____
_____
_____
_____
_____
_____
_____
_____
_____
_____
_____

OFFER TANGIBLE SUPPORT

When a friend experiences loss, daily tasks can feel overwhelming. Your friend may feel overwhelmingly sad or have trouble getting out of bed. Tasks such as cooking dinner may feel heavy and daunting. She may have a hard time making plans or remembering appointments. Be a good student of your friend, and seek tangible ways that you can serve her. Sample ideas may include:

- Cook her dinner. Bring an extra meal that she can freeze for later. Buy groceries for her.

- Watch her older children so that she can attend doctor's appointments or take a nap.

- Help her with any challenges to her calendar or schedule.

- Check in with the father to see how he is processing the grief.

- Mow the lawn.

- Give a gift card for groceries.

- Write a letter with Scripture verses and a note of encouragement that says, "I'm praying these verses with you."

- Make her a gift basket with items such as:

    ○ A candle

    ○ A necklace to remember the baby

- A journal

- A handwritten letter

• Help her identify a trusted biblical counselor, if needed.

• Pray for her and with her.

• Regularly ask how she is doing, even months after the miscarriage, stillbirth, or infant loss.

• _____

(Fill in the blanks to brainstorm practical ways to help your friend.)

• _____
• _____
• _____
• _____
• _____
• _____
• _____
• _____
• _____
• _____
• _____

How to Help Those Who Have Experienced Loss

MENTION THE BABY'S NAME

After a miscarriage, stillbirth, or infant loss, moms often feel the need to grieve quickly and quietly. They don't want to bother others with their grief, and their sadness seems to make everyone around them uncomfortable.

One simple way to love your friend is by mentioning the baby's name. Ask if it is hard for your friend to talk about the baby, and tell her that you would love to be a listening ear if she wants to talk. As you build this relationship, you may find opportunities to ask when she misses the baby most and what hopes she had for the baby. Consider asking questions such as, "What dreams did you have for _____ (say baby's name) or for your life as a mom? Do you ever think about what the baby would have been like?"

Listening to or crying with your friend can be a meaningful way to love her.

Do not be afraid to mention the baby, as often a grieving mom wants to talk about her baby, but she doesn't want to make you feel uncomfortable. Mentioning the baby by name can be a way to say that you also remember the baby she lost.

One simple way to love your friend is by mentioning the baby's name.

Listening to or crying with your friend can be a meaningful way to love her.

WHAT NOT TO SAY

It is very common for a woman who has experienced pregnancy or infant loss to receive a plethora of insensitive comments. If your friend is processing her grief due to miscarriage, stillbirth, or infant loss, be compassionate. Do not ask invasive questions, and when sensitive information is offered, do not gossip that information to others or betray her trust. Rather, enter into her grief, and cry with her.

If your friend experiences pregnancy or infant loss, do not say the following to her:

- *"At least... At least you know you can get pregnant. At least you have other children at home. At least you can sleep in on the weekends without a little baby around."* It is painful to lose a child. When a well-meaning friend tries to discount that pain with "at least" sentences, it can be very hurtful. It may make your friend think that you do not understand her pain and that she cannot process her grief with you in the future.

- *"Maybe there was going to be something wrong with the baby."* In the aftermath of death, try not to encourage your friend to look on the bright side too soon. Let her grieve the loss of her baby without making assumptions as to why this death is a blessing in disguise. When we try to find blessings through tragedy, it often makes a grieving friend feel like she must hide her true emotions or that she cannot be sad for the loss of her baby.

- *"Don't you have enough kids already?"* Children are a blessing from the Lord, and each life is a precious gift. Try not to judge the loss as a bullet that was dodged, but see it as a death to be grieved.

- *"So, when are you going to have more kids? Have you considered adoption?"* In the midst of grief, many people ask invasive and unhelpful questions. Do not ask personal questions like these ones, unless you are specifically invited to do so.

- *"Are you pregnant again?"* You may have suspicions that your friend is pregnant again after you notice her avoiding certain activities or not drinking alcohol. Even if this is the case, do not ask your friend if she is pregnant. This may be an invasive question, especially after your friend has already experienced the loss of a child. Let your friend share the news with you when she is ready.

- *"Maybe God is punishing you for _____ (an abortion, sexual sin in the past, etc.)."* God is merciful and forgives us for our sin. When we condemn others, we are not emulating the love and compassion of God.

- *"Did you exercise too much? Did you eat any foods you weren't supposed to have?"* After a loss, you may desire to help "problem-solve" so that your friend does not experience loss again. While your motives may be pure, do not ask questions that would suggest that the death is your friend's fault.

- *"Don't worry, you'll get pregnant again."* We do not know the future. While you may be trying to help your friend feel better, such platitudes are based on empty promises and are unhelpful.

Instead of offering trite platitudes or encouraging her to look on the bright side, consider one of the suggestions on pages 156–157.

Be a good student of your friend, and seek tangible ways that you can serve her.

WHAT TO SAY

- *"I'm so sorry. I wish there was something I could do to erase your pain, but I want you to know that I'm crying with you and grieving the loss of this baby with you."* We can express our love and concern for a friend by acknowledging her pain and offering a listening ear as she processes her loss.

- *"Do you want to talk about it?"* or *"Is it hard for you to talk about?"* Follow your friend's lead, and give her an opportunity to share about her grief. Often we can be afraid to bring up the loss of a loved one in fear that we will remind our friend of her loss and make her sad. But in reality, someone who has experienced the death of a baby is often thinking about her child. She likely desires to share what's on her heart, but she doesn't want to make you feel uncomfortable. If your friend wants to talk, give her space to lament and process the disappointment of dreams deferred. Give your friend the opportunity to share her thoughts and fears with you if she desires to do so.

- *"Can I bring you a meal or mow your yard?"* or *"I'm bringing you a meal on Wednesday. Do you have any allergies?"* Perceive the need, and follow through on acts of service that give your friend the time to grieve.

- *"I'm praying for you, and I want you to know that I'm here if you ever want to talk or cry."* Be available as a compassionate, listening ear.

- Mention the baby by name. By mentioning the baby's name, we show our friend that we recognize and remember the life of her sweet baby. We value her child's life, and we can honor our friends by mentioning their baby's name in conversation.

- Cry with your friend. Sometimes the best way to love our friends is to enter into the pain and cry with them.

- *"Are there any times of the week that are particularly hard for you?"* Send your friend a text to tell her that you're praying for her at that time of day.

- *"What is your grief like these days?"* Grief comes in waves. Although it may have been months or years since your friend lost her baby, she may still grieve the loss. Follow up with her regularly, and give her the opportunity to share her story with you.

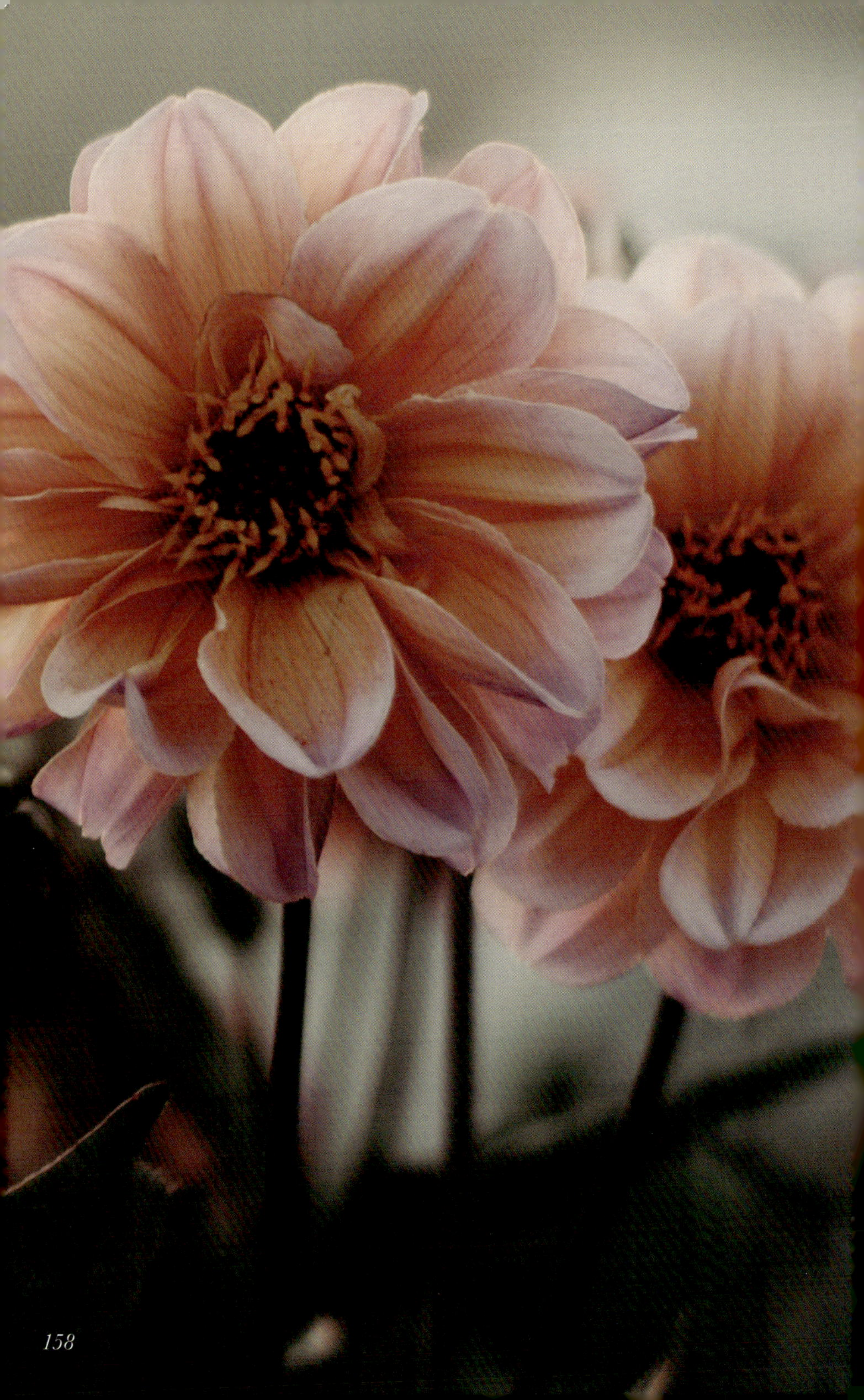

Although we cannot bring true peace and healing to our friends' souls, God can.

08.

Hope for the Future

"We know there is another due date coming — a day when God is coming to restore the world."

HOPE FOR THE FUTURE

One day, our pain will cease. God will return and right every wrong. There will be no more tears, barrenness, miscarriage, or death. God will wipe every tear and heal every hurt. He will restore the whole world and fill us with unspeakable joy, peace, and love. We'll no longer have confusion about medical decisions because all will be right. We won't need doctors because we'll never be sick. Read again the words of Revelation 21:1–7 about our future hope:

> Then I saw a new heaven and a new earth; for the first heaven and the first earth had passed away, and the sea was no more. I also saw the holy city, the new Jerusalem, coming down out of heaven from God, prepared like a bride adorned for her husband.
>
> Then I heard a loud voice from the throne: Look, God's dwelling is with humanity, and he will live with them. They will be his peoples, and God himself will be with them and will be their God. He will wipe away every tear from their eyes. Death will be no more; grief, crying, and pain will be no more, because the previous things have passed away.
>
> Then the one seated on the throne said, "Look, I am making everything new." He also said, "Write, because these words are faithful and true." Then he said to me, "It is done! I am the Alpha and the Omega, the beginning and the end. I will freely give to the thirsty from the spring of the water of life. The one who conquers will inherit these things, and I will be his God, and he will be my son.

One day, we'll be reunited with loved ones and rejoice together in our Savior's love. Although we feel the burden of pain, sorrow, and loss today, we look forward to the future when all will be made right. He is coming again to redeem and restore the world. We will finally be home. We can press into God in our grief because we know there is another due date coming—a day when God is coming to restore the world. On this day, there will be no more death but only everlasting life, peace, fulfillment, and joy for those who trust Him. He will make it right.

My Hope is Built on Nothing Less

My hope is built on nothing less
than Jesus' blood and righteousness;
I dare not trust the sweetest frame,
but wholly lean on Jesus' name.
On Christ, the solid Rock, I stand;
all other ground is sinking sand.

When darkness veils His lovely face,
I rest on His unchanging grace;
in ev'ry high and stormy gale
my anchor holds within the veil.
On Christ, the solid Rock, I stand;
all other ground is sinking sand.

His oath, His covenant, His blood
support me in the 'whelming flood;
when all around my soul gives way
He then is all my hope and stay.
On Christ, the solid Rock, I stand;
all other ground is sinking sand.

When He shall come with trumpet sound,
O may I then in Him be found,
dressed in His righteousness alone,
faultless to stand before the throne.
On Christ, the solid Rock, I stand;
all other ground is sinking sand.

Hope for the Future

God will wipe every tear and heal every hurt.

Hope for the Future / 165

God desires to bring healing, hope, and purpose out of your suffering.